A Case Study of the Factors in the Development of Spanish Linguistic Accuracy and Oral Communication Skills

A CASE STUDY OF THE FACTORS IN THE DEVELOPMENT OF SPANISH LINGUISTIC ACCURACY AND ORAL COMMUNICATION SKILLS

Motivation and Extended Interaction
in the Study Abroad Context

Christina Isabelli-García

Mellen Studies in Education
Volume 99

The Edwin Mellen Press
Lewiston•Queenston•Lampeter

Library of Congress Cataloging-in-Publication Data

Isabelli-García, Christina.
 A case study of the factors in the development of Spanish linguistic accuracy and oral communication skills : motivation and extended interaction in the study abroad context / Christina Isabelli-García.
  p. cm. -- (Mellen studies in education ; v. 99)
 [Includes bibliographical references and indexes.]
 ISBN 0-7734-6348-8
 1. Second language acquisition--Case studies. 2. Oral communication--Case studies. 3. Spanish language--Acquisition--Case studies. I. Title. II. Mellen studies in education (Lewiston, N.Y.) ; v. 99.

P118.2.I85 2004
468'.0071--dc22

                                2004042678

This is volume 99 in the continuing series
Mellen Studies in Education
Volume 99 ISBN 0-7734-6348-8
MSE Series ISBN 0-88946-935-0

A CIP catalog record for this book is available from the British Library

Front cover: *El Sol del futuro*, print by César Valverde, 1984

Copyright © 2004 Christina Isabelli-García

All rights reserved. For information contact

    The Edwin Mellen Press   The Edwin Mellen Press
    Box 450   Box 67
    Lewiston, New York   Queenston, Ontario
    USA 14092-0450   CANADA L0S 1L0

      The Edwin Mellen Press, Ltd.
      Lampeter, Ceredigion, Wales
      UNITED KINGDOM SA48 8LT

    Printed in the United States of America

TABLE OF CONTENTS

List of Illustrations	vii
Preface - Barbara F. Freed	ix
Acknowledgements	xiii
Introduction: Issues, Challenges and Assumptions about Study Abroad	1
Literature Review	6
Language Development While Abroad	7
Research on linguistic acquisition	7
Research on the development of oral communication skills	11
Interaction in the Host Culture by Program Participants	14
Chapter 1: Study Abroad and Theories in Second Language Acquisition	19
Theories on Input and Interaction	19
Theories on Motivation, Social Networks, and Acculturation	22
The Role of Ethnographic Research	31
Research Questions	32
Chapter 2: Participants, and the Data Collection and Analysis Process	35
Learner Participants	35
Data Collection Instruments	39
The simulated oral proficiency interview	39
The informal interviews	42
Diary entries and network contact logs	42
Data Analyses	44
Simulated oral proficiency interview	44
Informal oral interviews	45
Classification of data: Linguistic accuracy	45
Classification of data: Oral communication skills	47
Diary entries	57
Network contact logs	58

Chapter 3: Quantitative Results and Analyses: Linguistic Accuracy and
Oral Communication Skills... 59
    Discussion of the Linguistic Development of the Group as a Whole....... 62
    Quantitative Results for Each Learner.. 68
        Stan's progress in linguistic accuracy and oral communication......... 68
        Tom's progress in linguistic accuracy and oral communication......... 71
        Mark's progress in linguistic accuracy and oral communication........ 77
        Sam's progress in linguistic accuracy and oral communication......... 82
        Jennifer's progress in linguistic accuracy and oral communication ... 86
    Discussion... 89
        Oral communication skills and linguistic development 89
    Summary... 93

Chapter 4: Qualitative Results and Analysis: Attitudes and Social
Networks.. 95
    Qualitative Analysis and Discussion for Each Learner........................... 98
        Stan's attitudes and social network... 98
        Tom's attitudes and social network... 106
        Mark's attitudes and social network.. 114
        Sam's attitudes and social network... 119
        Jennifer's attitudes and social network... 125
    Summary... 132

Chapter 5: Concluding Remarks.. 133
    Findings.. 135
        What kind of development is seen in the learners' linguistic
        accuracy in Spanish while abroad?... 135
        What kind of development is seen in the learners' oral
        communication skills in Spanish while abroad?............................... 137
        What individual factors enter into the success of development?......... 141

What is the minimal amount of time students should spend
   abroad to benefit linguistically from the experience............................ 144
   Conclusions 145
   Directions for future research... 150

Appendix A: Background Questionnaires... 153
Appendix B: Interview Materials... 154
Appendix C: Network Contact Logs.. 155
Bibliography... 157
Indices 169

LIST OF ILLUSTRATIONS

Figures

1	High density, Closed Personal Network Structure	24
2	Low Density, Open Personal Network Structure	25
3	Low Density Network Showing First and Second Order Zones	27
4	Stan's Language Choice Over Time in Social Situations	102
5	Stan's (X) First and Second Order Zone Social Networks	103
6	Tom's Language Choice Over Time in Social Situations	108
7	Tom's (X) First and Second Order Zone Social Networks	111
8	Mark's (X) First and Second Order Zone Social Networks	115
9	Mark's Language Choice Over Time in Social Situations	119
10	Sam's Language Choice Over Time in Social Situations	122
11	Sam's (X) First and Second Order Zone Social Networks	123
12	Jennifer's (X) First and Second Order Zone Social Networks	127
13	Jennifer's Language Choice Over Time in Social Situations	130

Tables

1	Simulated Oral Proficiency Interview Ratings	61
2	Average Linguistic Improvement (ai) in Percentages	65
3	Average Slopes (ß) of Development for All Learners	66
4	Stan's Linguistic Accuracy in Percentages	69
5	Stan's Oral Communication Skills	71
6	Tom's Linguistic Accuracy in Percentages	72
7	Tom's Oral Communication Skills	76
8	Mark's Linguistic Accuracy in Percentages	78
9	Mark's Oral Communication Skills	79
10	Sam's Linguistic Accuracy in Percentages	83
11	Sam's Oral Communication Skills	85
12	Jennifer's Linguistic Accuracy in Percentages	86

13	Jennifer's Oral Communication Skills	88
14	Stan's First and Second Order Zone Social Networks	103
15	Tom's First and Second Order Zone Social Networks	111
16	Mark's First and Second Order Zone Social Network	114
17	Sam's First and Second Order Zone Social Networks	123
18	Jennifer's First and Second Order Zone Social Networks	127

PREFACE

In the early 1990s a number of second language acquisition (SLA) scholars began to explore the linguistic consequences of study abroad experiences. The reasons for their interest in this topic were many but perhaps most important was the fact that there was little, if any, robust data which documented the prevailing belief in the advantages of so called "immersion" in the native speech community. Since that time the field has expanded, just as Ferguson predicted, so that research that focuses on different contexts of second language (L2) learning -- specifically, comparisons of language learning in the formal language classroom, intensive domestic immersion and study abroad settings -- has become a major subfield of SLA research (xi, 1995).

Studies of this type have focused on different languages (French, German, Spanish, Japanese, Russian), have looked at short term (summer), academic semester or year long experiences and have begun to compare gains in fluency, lexicon, syntax, communication strategies and sociolinguistic appropriateness for students who live and study in these various contexts of learning. Some of this work has also begun to look beyond actual language learning to features of the language learning environment itself.

As I articulated in 1995, numerous questions remained before us if we were to better understand the L2 learning process as well as the sociocultural impact of study abroad experiences on student L2 learning. Prominent among these questions were those that sought to measure and evaluate the quality and extent of student social contact and language use while abroad (18, 1995). Recent work (Collentine, 2004; Dewey, 2004; Díaz-Campos, 2004; Freed, Segalowitz & Dewey, 2004; Lafford, 2004; Lazar, 2004; Polanyi, 1995; Segalowitz & Freed, 2004; Wilkinson, 1998) has sharpened our insights into the comparative advantages of L2 study in various contexts and the relationship between in and out of class language use. It is in precisely this respect that Christina Isabelli-

García's book brings yet additional data to deepen our understanding of the relationship between what students do while abroad and how this behavior may influence the extent and type of language gain in the study abroad context.

A Case Study of the Factors in the Development of Spanish Linguistic Accuracy: Motivation and Extended Interaction in the Study Abroad Context is a particularly welcomed book to the literature on context of learning, specifically study in an education abroad context. To begin with Isabelli-García carefully builds on the groundwork of prior research in the field, providing a useful point of comparison with earlier work. In addition, she opens new areas of exploration into the relationship of social interaction and various aspects of language gain. In this fashion, she begins to fill in some of the lacunae which existed between understanding second language learning itself and the extralinguistic influences that inevitably affect the form and content of such learning.

The richness of the case studies that form the basis of Isabelli-García's work is based on careful analyses of linguistic growth – from the perspective of oral proficiency, grammatical accuracy and functional usage – and individual patterns of social use. In particular, Isabelli-García explores the role of student motivation, attitudes and the extent to which these qualities correlate with superior development of oral communication skills and linguistic accuracy.

In reading this volume we are introduced to 5 prototypical American undergraduates and the roads they travel in embracing a second language and culture. As L2 scholars and teachers, each of the student's paths is abstractly known to us but never before have we had an opportunity to follow intimately the social networks that individual students establish, their cultural awareness, their personal feelings about their experiences and how these feelings and networks interact in the development of their L2 language skills. Along the way we are confronted with surprises as well as affirmations of some intuitive and/or documented beliefs about what most favors language gain, at home or abroad.

Isabelli-García's insightful analyses provide further support for prior research that has demonstrated that the mere use of a second language outside of the classroom context does not necessarily guarantee superior language gain of all types. Prior suggestions that it is not only quantity but quality of interaction that most favors language gain is reinforced, as is the fact that language gain cannot be measured simply by traditional means of assessment. We observe that "grammar" may temporarily decline while discourse skills are enhanced, that students' narrative abilities may excel at the same time that we see their ability to use a prescribed syntactic form backslide.

Isabelli-García's work has charted new challenges for those of us interested in the role of context of learning on L2 use. Her detailed case studies provide a model for more extensive research for those interested in the complex interaction of social network, cognitive ability, individual differences and context of learning. In years to come, we will surely look back to this fine work as a milestone in the development of research on language learning in a study abroad context and an important contribution to the profession.

Barbara F. Freed, *Department of Modern Languages*
Carnegie Mellon University
August 2004

ACKNOWLEDGMENTS

Several individuals have contributed to this work at various stages. To James Alstrum, the professor who first interested me in study abroad during my undergraduate studies at Illinois State University. I wish to thank those at the University of Iowa and the University of Texas at Austin and that have encouraged, guided, and shaped my graduate education, especially Judith Liskin-Gasparro, Chiyo Nishida, and Dale A. Koike. Also Eton Churchill, Margaret A. DuFon at California State University at Chico, and the reviewers of *Frontiers* that gave helpful comments on key portions of the book.

I am especially indebted to Barbara Freed at Carnegie Mellon University, who gave valuable encouragement for the project from the early stages of writing through the reviewing and editing. Her suggestions were always timely and valuable. A special thanks also goes to the study abroad participants.

To Cassie for always being there, sharing, advising, and driving me forward. To Anthony for giving grounded opinions and, of course, adding humor to my life. To Mom and Dad for offering me many sound reference points that serve as a secure guide along life's path.

Finally, I add special thanks to, Arturo, for being an unconditional source of encouragement, motivation, and to Sofia for giving me a sense of balance.

INTRODUCTION: ISSUES, CHALLENGES AND ASSUMPTIONS ABOUT STUDY ABROAD

> *Applicants...have often fallen prey to the seductive illusion that eating the native bread and drinking the favorite local café beverage will somehow enhance their fluency.*
>
> Day (1987, p. 262)

As a professor of a foreign language I frequently recommend my students to study abroad for a semester to take advantage of the opportunity to interact with the native speakers to improve their language skills. Many are nervous about the idea of spending a semester in a foreign country and totally emerging themselves in a non-familiar city, bringing back my own memories of knowing nothing about the host culture, its people, and wondering if I would survive in the new environment with my limited language abilities. As can be seen from the title, this book addresses what happens to a student's language when s/he goes abroad. I became interested in this subject when I went abroad for the first time to Mexico to learn Spanish and after the experience, I wondered why some of my fellow study-abroaders seemed to have advanced minimally in their language skills whereas others had, and in the worst case scenario, why one student could not make it through the entirety of the semester and decided to quit the program. I made an observation at that point that some of them had integrated into circles of friendships with Mexican natives and others had not ventured outside of their safety net of American friends, forgoing valuable social interaction with native speakers. Their social networks were very different from each other. This same observation has been made in language learning research. As cited in Peirce (1995, p. 13):

> It is through language that a person negotiates a sense of self within and across different sites at different points in time, and it is through language that a person gains access to -- or is denied access to -- powerful social networks that give learners the opportunity to speak. (Heller, 1987)

This study tries to re-create that experience I had many years ago as a study abroad student, with the aim of finding out what learners do differently abroad and how it may affect their acquisition of the target language. Therefore, this research examines the impact of a one-semester study abroad experience in Argentina on the second language acquisition of five American university Spanish learners. The goal is three-fold: (1) to measure development of linguistic accuracy of (a) tense selection, (b) aspect selection, (c) subject-verb agreement, and (d) gender-number agreement; (2) to measure development of skills in performing the functions of narration, description, and opinion; and (3) to relate patterns of social contact via analysis of social network logs to development in oral ability as measured by gains in linguistic accuracy and oral communication skills over time. I submit that the two vital factors that lead to acquisition gains in the study abroad context are motivation and significant target language interaction with native speakers in social networks. I show through qualitative and quantitative data that those who had high motivation were those that had more extended networks, which correlated with gains in linguistic accuracy and development in functions of oral ability.

Research has shown that immersion in the target culture is of great value to the learner's second language acquisition, especially in improvement of oral production ability (Brecht, Davidson, & Ginsberg, 1993; Carroll, 1967; Freed, 1990a, b; Howard, 2001; Isabelli, 2003; Kaplan, 1989; Lennon, 1990b; Liskin-Gasparro & Urdaneta, 1995; Milleret, 1990; Polanyi, 1995) but there is also conflicting negative evidence that study abroad leads to grammatical progress

(Collentine, 2004; DeKeyser, 1991; Freed 1995a; Moehle, 1984; Möhle & Raupach, 1983; Regan, 1995). Nevertheless, few studies have addressed the changes of specific linguistic aspects, such as aspect and tense selection and subject-verb and gender-number agreement, that occur during the study abroad experience and how they develop.

Another area of second language development that is growing in research, besides the general development of oral production ability and increases in specific areas of linguistic accuracy, is that of development in certain oral communication skills may that include the use of specific speech functions, production, flow and quantity of speech (DeKeyser, 1991; Díaz-Campos, 2004; Freed, 1995b; Lafford, 1995, 2004; Liskin-Gasparro, 1996, Segalowitz & Freed, 2004). Several of the studies use some sort of oral proficiency test to evaluate learners' development before and after the study abroad program. The very well defined scoring criteria of the American Council on the Teaching of Foreign Languages (ACTFL) Proficiency Guidelines (2000) single out Function, or what the user does with language, as the most crucial element in oral proficiency assessment among the other components of content, context, accuracy, and text type. Although there exists much research on pre- and post-program proficiency gains, there is little documentation that describes specific development in the learner's oral communication skill of performing functions in a month-by-month observation. This study analyzes the development of these oral communication skills in instances of functions by the learner and relates them to patterns of social contact.

Freed (1995a) points out that even though "previous investigations have laid the groundwork for fruitful explorations of the effects of study abroad experiences on the language proficiency of those who participate in these programs...numerous questions remain to be answered by carefully-controlled empirical studies" (p. 16). One of the many theoretical and practical questions she asks concerns the actual linguistic benefits of time spent in a study abroad program. She poses the question, "Is it improved accent, greater use of idioms, improved accuracy, expanded discourse strategies, greater improved listening comprehension, improved oral or written communication, greater syntactic complexity, or broader sociolinguistic range?" (p.17). I approach the issue by analyzing two of Freed's (1995a) topics of study: the kind of development that is seen in the learner's (a) improved linguistic accuracy; and (b) improved oral communication skills in the language functions throughout the study abroad program.

To study the development of a learner's linguistic accuracy and oral communication skills while abroad also implies that research be done on the extralinguistic factors that may influence the acquisition process. Studies that examine learners' behavior and motivation in the host culture and link it directly to the development of their linguistic capabilities and oral skills will disprove that going abroad is just a chance to do little work and that one will magically become a fluent speaker simply because one is surrounded by the target language.

In second language acquisition, it is easy to claim that a learner will be successful with the proper motivation. According to Brown (1995, p. 152), motivation is commonly thought of as an inner drive, impulse, emotion, or desire that moves one to a particular action. In more technical terms, motivation refers to the choices people make as to what experiences or goals they will approach or avoid, and the degree of effort they will exert in that respect. Ellis (1998, p. 75) indicates that studies of motivation in second language acquisition have identified various kinds of complementary learner motivation orientation: instrumental; integrative; resultative; and intrinsic. It should be noted that categorization of learner motivation is not black and white, but rather motivation represents a continuum of orientations. For more elaborate discussion on motivation see (Gardner & Lambert, 1972; Gardner & MacIntyre, 1991; Gardner & Smythe, 1975).

Instrumental motivation embraces sociocultural, socioeducational, and socio-psychological issues like belonging in a group, receiving affection, and identifying with the foreign language community. On the other hand, instrumental orientation deals with the utilitarian use of the language for personal gain, like finding a job, or furthering a career. Resultative motivation occurs when learners who experience success or failure in learning become more or less motivated to learn. That is, motivation may cause second language achievement; however, it is also possible that motivation is a result of learning. It may be that many learners do not hold distinct attitudes, positive or negative, towards the target-language group. In this case, intrinsic motivation involves the arousal and maintenance of curiosity and can fluctuate as a result of such factors as learners' particular interests.

I must note here that based on Peirce's (1995) research, she states that, "Such conceptions of motivation...do not capture the complex relationship between relations of power, identity, and language learning" (p. 17). Rather, she postulates that if the learners have some sort of "investment" to learn a second language, "they do so with the understanding that they will acquire a wider range of symbolic and material resources" (p. 17). With investment meaning that "the language learner as having a complex social identity and multiple desires" (pp. 17-18). The notion of motivation I use in this investigation coincides with both Peirce's notion of investment and with those notions of motivation (Gardner & Lambert, 1972; Gardner & MacIntyre, 1991; Gardner & Smythe, 1975), but especially with Peirce's (1995). I agree with her viewpoint that "motivation is not a fixed personality trait but must be understood with reference to social relations of power that create the possibilities for language learners to speak" and that "students' social identities are complex, multiple, and subject to change" (p. 26).

Motivation is clearly a complex phenomenon but an important question remains: how does the environment in which the learners interact create, foster, and maintain motivation? Without studies that focus on the interdependency of motivation and interaction in the environment and language acquisition, second language researchers cannot grasp the totality of the effect that the study abroad learners' perseverance has over their own language acquisition process. Freed (1998) states, "Unfortunately...relatively little scholarly attention has been devoted to documenting changes in the communicative language proficiency of students who have studied abroad" (p. 31). Through research that focuses on language change in a native speech community rather than in the foreign language classroom, evidence can be found to support hypotheses that cross-cultural understanding can aid second language acquisition as well as to support the universality of theories regarding an order of morpheme acquisition or a sequential development in such syntactic areas as tense, aspect, and agreement. Moreover, due to the growing participation of learners in study abroad programs, there is a need for data that can empirically show parents, teachers, and learners the kinds of development in linguistic and oral communication skills that can be expected from spending time abroad and the elements that may influence this development.

Literature Review

For those readers that are not acquainted with the area of second language acquisition (SLA), I must note that there is not one single theory that encompasses all aspects of this field. Instead, there exist several theories. This fact has sometimes led researchers outside of the field to conclude that SLA study is a process of only exploration and speculation rather than one of discovery and proof, as noted by Block (1996). He and other researchers do acknowledge, however, that SLA is multidimensional in nature. And although SLA is a relatively new field of research, it certainly does not lack studies that have discovered and proven certain claims about language acquisition.

With the aim of outlining the role of this book in the field of SLA, this next section surveys the inconsistencies that other researchers and I have found in

SLA with respect to the study abroad context. The first subsection surveys research on learners' language development while abroad, including studies that focus on linguistic acquisition and development in oral communication skills while the second reviews research on interaction in the host culture by program participants.

Language Development While Abroad

It is accepted by educators that language development normally occurs during a study abroad over a given period of time, but a majority use anecdotes or commonsensical arguments to 'prove' this point. In 1967, Carroll guided one of the pioneer studies that analyzes the benefits of study abroad showing that time spent abroad is one of the predictors of target language ability. After Carroll's study there has been much research carried out on language performance during the study abroad experience that cover a gamut of aspects. Here, however, I focus only on the development of specific linguistic features during study abroad.

Research on linguistic acquisition

The work of Brecht and Robinson (1993) and Brecht, Davidson, and Ginsberg (1993) encompass a broad view of the acquisition process. They statistically analyze the relationship between learner characteristics and pre- and post-program assessments of speaking, listening, and reading abilities and find that study abroad is an effective context for undergraduate students to learn to speak Russian. They also conclude that study abroad learners with higher levels of pre-program reading ability display greater progress in speaking and listening skills. But, according to Freed (1995a), Brecht and Robinson (1993) and Brecht, Davidson, and Ginsberg's (1993) sole reliance on the pre- and post-program test scores to measure linguistic skills reveals little about qualitative changes that occur in the learners' language ability, even though a strong positive correlation exists between linguistic growth and study abroad.

DeKeyser (1991) states that the results of several studies (Moehle, 1984; Raupach, 1983, 1984) indicate that grammar does not change in any noticeable way as a result of several months spent in the host culture in terms of frequency of mistakes or length and syntactic complexity of sentences. DeKeyser's (1991) own investigation of study abroad learners in Spain during a one-semester stay compares the language skills of American students who spend a semester abroad to those of American students who learn the language in the home country. He finds that there are no significant differences between the two types of learning situations that would designate one as a better learning environment over the other and further concluded that study abroad learners undoubtedly gain in fluency and expand their vocabulary. No characterization is given as to what entails a gain in fluency, however.

A study that seems to identify specifics in the linguistic development of learners in the study abroad context is that of Lapkin, Hart, and Swain (1995). The investigators evaluate the experience of over a hundred English-speaking learners during a three-month exchange program in Quebec and examine gains in French language ability, as indicated by test results and learners' self assessments. The test focuses on the use of the past and conditional tense, sociolinguistic appropriateness, spelling and grammar errors, and use of politeness markers. Although the data show that learners with initially lower French language ability make greater gains as a result of submersion in a French environment, no specific information is given regarding what linguistic aspects improve during the stay abroad.

Huebner's (1995) comparison study of learners of Japanese in an intensive summer study abroad program and those in the foreign language classroom does not show specific language development, as do the studies of DeKeyser (1986), but rather shows trends that differentiate the two groups. These trends include: (a) the positive effect that the study abroad program has on acquisition of literacy in the target language; (b) an indication that opportunities for informal, out-of-class contact *may* encourage a willingness to produce more language; and (c) the suggestion that some aspects of language use (such as the use of zero anaphora[1] versus full noun phrases for continuous topics in narrative retelling to maintain topics) need not be taught.

Other researchers that use data collected in the native speech community and contribute to the literature on the development of certain linguistic elements are those of Collentine (2004), Díaz-Campos (2004), Howard (2001), Isabelli (2004), Lennon (1990b), Ryan and Lafford (1992), and Lafford and Ryan (1996).

Collentine (2004) analyzes data collected from a pre- and post-semester oral proficiency interview (OPI) from learners of Spanish in an at home context and in a study abroad context. The results indicate that the at home context facilitate more development on discrete grammatical and lexical features but conclude that the study abroad group achieve better narrative abilities and produce more semantically dense language. The conclusions suggest that study abroad learner's grammatical accuracy is not much better than before the program but that the same learners are perceived as being able to "tell a story" and getting "their point across" better (p. 245). Background information that may have effected this surprising difference are the following: the pre-SAT II Spanish test scores placed the at home group at a slightly higher university-level Spanish instruction in the US than the study abroad group (beginning of the third semester vs. the middle of the second semester) and that the mode pre-OPI score for the at home group was Intermediate-Mid whereas for the study abroad group it was a bit lower, Intermediate-Low.

Díaz-Campos (2004), using the same participant group as Collentine (2004) analyzes phonological data collected from the Language Contact Profile (Freed, Dewey, & Segalowitz, 2004) at the beginning and at the end of the program along with a speech sample collected from a short read-aloud text. He finds that both groups (study abroad and at home) show the same outcome at the end of the treatment period (p. 270). The conclusion is again surprising since the study abroad student did not outperform the at home language learner as would commonly be expected.

As cited in Collentine (2004), Howard (2001) and (1990b) find positive effects of the study abroad context upon examining particular grammatical structures. Howard (2001) reports that, while learners of French in a study abroad context struggle to make native-like associations between lexical and inflectional aspect, they make important gains in their abilities to generate narratives with past-tense markers, as Collentine (2004) above. Lennon's (1990b) data corroborate the benefit of the study abroad context. The conclusions show that German students of English developed increased syntactic complexity.

Isabelli (2004) investigates the treatment of null subject pronouns, verb-subject inversion, and that-*trace* construction by second language intermediate learners of Spanish in Spain. She provides evidence to answer whether there is a significant difference on grammaticality judgment test scores on the three structures from 0 to 4 months and from 4 to 9 months in the study abroad setting. Isabelli concludes that the most salient and least abstract syntactic feature (Null Subject) is acquired before onset of study abroad, that verb-subject inversion, which is somewhat salient and not abstract, is acquired within 4 months, and the acquisition of the least salient and most abstract feature, that-*trace*, is seen after 4 months.

Ryan and Lafford (1992) provide data from a study abroad environment to support prior assertions about natural stages in the acquisition of the Spanish copula ser and estar 'to be'. The authors come to conclusions similar to those of VanPatten (1985), differing in that the latter study was based on data gathered in a foreign language classroom setting. The difference between VanPatten's (1985) classroom learners and Ryan and Lafford's (1992) study abroad learners is that the latter were exposed to more natural input than can be provided in the classroom. In a parallel study, Lafford and Ryan (1996) evaluated the development of form and function of the prepositions por and para 'for' at different levels of oral production in the interlanguage of one-semester study abroad learners in Spain. The authors proposed an order of acquisition of functions normally assigned to these prepositions by native Spanish speakers.

According to Freed (1995a), studies such as those just mentioned, "represent an important step in the direction of a more complete understanding of the impact of study abroad experiences on students' language learning" (p. 12). In addition, future research needs to clarify contradictions seen in study abroad language acquisition literature. As stated earlier, DeKeyser (1991), Huebner (1995), Moehle (1984), and Raupach (1983, 1984) indicate that specific language development does not change in the host culture after several months abroad but DeKeyser (1991) does conclude that a gain is seen in fluency. On the other hand, Lapkin, Hart, and Swain (1995) show that study abroad learners make gains as a result of submersion in a host environment. It must be noted that the conclusions of several of these studies (Huebner, 1995; Lapkin, Hart, & Swain, 1995) are based on data collected in an intensive summer, or three-month language program, leading the reader to generalize their conclusions to learners in a semester- or year-long study abroad program.

Research on the development of oral communication skills

Compared to the research on linguistic development abroad, research on the development of oral communication skills, which include the use of specific speech functions as well as flow and quantity of speech, but not communication strategies, is limited.

Lafford's (1995) study investigates the use of communicative strategies (fillers and connectors, backchannel signals, repairs/repeats and the addition of information) among study abroad and at home students using a role-play situation on an exit oral proficiency interview (OPI). She concludes that although "the study abroad experience broadens the repertoire of communicative strategies of L2 [second language] learners and makes them better conversationalists" (p. 119) the "SA [study abroad] group employed significantly fewer CSs [communication strategies] than the AH [at home] group" (2004, p. 209). Although not investigated in her 1995 study, Lafford notes that when compared to the at home students, the study abroad students showed more facility with the language as evidenced through few pauses while groping for words, shorter pauses, and a faster rate of speed of their speech, making them "sound more fluent" (p. 111).

Segalowitz & Freed (2004) make similar conclusions using data collected from study abroad learners. Using pre- and post-test oral proficiency variables, they conclude that learners in this context made significant gains in oral ability whereas learners in the at home context did not. This was seen with respect to pre- and post-test differences on two general oral ability variables (OPI and longest speaking turn) and on three oral fluency measures (speech rate, mean length of speech run not containing filled pauses, and longest fluent run not containing silent hesitations or filled pauses). Freed (1995b) also concludes in her investigation of 30 French learners that "rate of speech is the only fluency feature which yields a significant difference between the At Home and Abroad groups" (p. 137). However, upon adding an additional participant group, that of the domestic immersion context (7 weeks during the summer), Freed, Segalowitz and Dewey (2004) conclude "the IM [immersion group] made significant gains in oral ability in terms of the total number of words spoken, in length of the longest turn, in rate of speech, and in speech fluidity based on a composite of fluidity measures" (p. 276) as compared to the study abroad students that demonstrated greater gains on several of the variables than did the foreign language classroom students but fewer than those in the immersion context (p. 276).

Examining data from recordings made in French by 12 advanced learners after their return from a year abroad, Towell, Hawkins, and Bazergui (1996) state that "as exposure to and practice of L2 increases so does fluency" (p. 98) and that "their uninterrupted or fluent speech runs tend also to be longer" (p. 142). The authors' overall conclusion is that these learners become more fluent as a result of their residence abroad.

More practitioners and administrators of educational programs want concrete evidence that shows what it takes to achieve an Intermediate or Advanced level of proficiency, which is usually the benchmark to pass oral proficiency tests in the target language. In recent years, various educational institutions have been implementing either oral proficiency interviews of simulated oral proficiency interviews in outcome-based curriculums, using interview tests as a requirement towards a degree. For example, the state of Texas requires an Advanced score on an oral proficiency test as one of the criteria for qualification to be an elementary, middle, or high school language or bilingual educator.

The revised ACTFL Proficiency Guidelines (Breiner-Sanders, Lowe, Miles, & Swender, 2000) list the criteria to rate the learners at different levels of proficiency and many communicative tasks are involved in a proficiency interview. The tasks include such speech functions as narrating, describing, hypothesizing, and supporting an opinion. Speech samples are rated for such specific qualities as organization, clarity of message, connectedness, accuracy of grammar, and comprehensibility, to name a few. According to my personal training as a simulated oral proficiency interview (SOPI) rater for four years, based on a modified form of the ACTFL Oral Proficiency Interview, the average learner's inability to adequately produce more advanced speech functions generally results in a non-passing score. This failure is due to the fact that these advanced speech functions may be difficult to achieve through on-campus classroom language learning alone. It is particularly surprising when veteran bilingual educators, and even heritage bilingual speakers, fail to pass the proficiency test due to their lack of practice of advanced level tasks during their language learning process or their daily routines. This difficulty was noted by a future examinee of the oral proficiency test in Texas in an on-line chat room (Spanish Teachers Chatboard, 2000):

> I must take the TOPT [Texas] oral proficiency test for certification in Spanish. HELP!!! Our District translator failed with a 50 the first try. Our professors say the failure rate is over 70 percent. With stats like that, I say anything you've seen on the test is of major importance to me. How can I pass which is made to be impossible to study for? The trial questions they print are nowhere near the actual questions according to my sources. Ayúdame, por favor.

To overcome this deficiency, some learners participate in oral proficiency test preparation courses that review strategies to structure and handle the more difficult advanced level tasks successfully. It is understandable then that oral proficiency testers and educational institutions that hope their learners will pass the test are curious as to what is necessary to become a more advanced level speaker. More research is needed that shows that development of those speech functions happens in the study abroad context, how it happens and, more importantly, if this development requires an extended stay abroad. This important research will support notions that a semester abroad may be a beneficial requirement of a successful curriculum for learners in foreign language studies.

Interaction in the Host Culture by Program Participants

Nearly 15 years after Schumann (1976) claimed that the environment in which the learners interact, the opportunities to use the language, and learners' attitudinal and motivational patterns all seem to directly influence their rate of acquisition, other investigations have agreed and disagreed with these conclusions. Freed (1995a) discusses the relationship between out-of-class contact and language acquisition and states that there is an untested assumption, but not well documented, that learners who most seek to use the target language will be the ones who ultimately make the most progress. Studies that produce supportive and contradictory evidence on this relationship are detailed here.

Phase II of Brecht, Davidson, and Ginsberg's (1993) study show a correlation between language gains and certain behavior in the target country. They reach the same conclusion as Schumann (1976); that is, that the environment has a direct influence on learners' rate of acquisition. Brecht et al. build on earlier work by giving a more detailed account of the social activities in which learners with a higher rate of acquisition engage. Milleret (1990) also concludes that diminishing the learners' contact with the host culture limits the opportunity for language practice. According to her study, cultural and linguistic input, the uncontrollable external factor for study abroad learners, is the basis for much of the learning that goes on outside of the classroom. Kaplan's (1989) survey of the amount of French used abroad by learners indicates that living with a family seems to provide more regular opportunities to use the target language as compared to living in dormitories.

Polanyi (1995) also studies how the environment affects language acquisition, but focuses on gender differences. Aptitude, educational background, and entrance skill levels among the subjects for this study were equal. As measured by standardized tests, the women's scores for listening and speaking skills did not improve as much as the men's scores during a Russian study abroad program. Polanyi attributes this difference to the quality and quantity of interactions the two groups had while abroad. While the men were learning to be "Russian language speakers" (p. 289) by discussing abstract topics such as music and politics, women were learning to be "women Russian language speakers" by learning how to deal with difficult and sometimes humiliating social encounters.

If and when intercultural relationships do occur between the language learner and the natives in the host country, many factors affect the amount and type of participation in these relationships over time. This is just one aspect of the complexity of language acquisition in the study abroad context. For example, in a study of Japanese and American intercultural relationships over a nine-month period, Krzic (1995, p. 90) finds two reasons for an increase in Japanese learners' social networks with Americans. First, the learners' improvement in language skills led to an increase of confidence: "many of them expressed being more comfortable meeting Americans because they could speak more and understand more English." The second was social, motivated by a "sense of urgency to meet friends due to the fact that the study abroad adventure was soon to end."

Freed (1995a, p. 6) points out recent contradictory evidence that suggests that informal, out-of-class contact, which presumably provides more linguistic input and obligates use of communicative strategies, does not necessarily enhance acquisition (DeKeyser, 1991; Freed, 1990b; Krashen & Seliger, 1976; Krashen, Seliger, & Harnett, 1974; Segalowitz & Freed, 2004; Spada, 1985, 1986), and may even impede second language acquisition (Higgs & Clifford, 1982). Freed (1990b) observed the social patterns of study abroad learners and concludes that out-of-class contact during a six-week period does not seem to influence oral proficiency as measured by the OPI. No change in growth of oral ability is noted from the effect of out-of-class contact on oral proficiency scores. Her claims do not support Schumann's (1976) original claim that the environment in which the learners interact seems to have a direct influence on the rate of acquisition. Freed's conclusions may differ due to the possibility that a six-week period is too short to show any measurable progress in L2 oral proficiency. DeKeyser's (1991) study also finds no significant difference between learners who learn the language in the classroom and those who learn the language abroad, and there are no significant differences between the two groups in explicit knowledge of the grammar and oral ability.

Segalowitz and Freed (2004) studied 22 learners studying abroad in Spain for one year and 19 at home Spanish students. Their results point to the fact that the increased opportunities available to study abroad learners do not necessarily result in oral ability gains over the semester. In other words the "amount of in-class and out-of-class contact appeared to have only a weak and indirect impact on oral gains" (p. 192).

> one can ask whether extracurricular use of the L2 had an impact on gains in oral performance ... the answer seems to be no...One would have expected that students who took advantage of the many opportunities to communicate with NSs [native speakers] in general, and with the home-stay family in particular, would have shown greater gains in oral performance...they did not... One explanation for this may be that the amount of contact was simply too little. (Segalowitz & Freed, 2004, pp. 192-193)

In trying to find an explanation for why students studying abroad for one year did not have sufficient interaction with the host culture, Segalowitz and Freed (2004) cite Frank (1997) and Wilkinson (1998). These authors suggest that "home-stay interactions may have consisted largely of short exchanges--greetings, simple requests, short formulaic exchanges (chit chat)--that resulted, if anything, in greater ability to communicate without necessarily holding the floor for a long time" (p. 193).

Pellegrino (1998) adds that learners assume that they will learn language from mere exposure to native speakers, what Wilkinson (1997) refers to as the "language myth." This fact is corroborated with Freed, Segalowitz and Dewey's (2004) conclusions that students in the study abroad context "reported using more English in out-of-class contact than they did using French" (p. 294) while living in Paris. Additionally, due to what Bacon (1995) attributes to culture shock and culture adaptation, the study abroad learners do not interact with their host as much as expected. Pellegrino (1998) concludes that this happens because of the learners' need to maintain "social psychological security." Wilkinson (1998, p. 32) goes a step further and justifies the function of an American peer group for a group studying abroad during an eight-month period in France.

> The formation of American peer groups seemed to serve an important function: it provided the confirmation of native identity necessary to enable the students to face the potentially threatening situations of linguistic and cultural difference...As participants begin to integrate into their new surroundings, boundaries between in- and out-groups became 'softer' and new cross-cultural identities develop, thereby diminishing the need for native-culture anchoring.

Nonetheless, studies have shown that the amount of contact with native speakers is an important factor in the acquisition of sociolinguistic and sociocultural knowledge (Lafford, 1995; Lapkin, Hart, & Swain, 1995; Marriot, 1995; Regan, 1995, 1998; Siegal, 1995). However, Freed, So, and Lazar's (2003) study cite Firth and Wagner (1997, p. 285) that "SLA research...fails to account for...sociolinguistic dimensions of language...and obviates insight into the nature of language, most centrally the language use of second or foreign language speakers."

As can be seen, one cannot generalize across studies of study abroad experiences and gains. There are inconsistencies in the research since claims are made based on different aspects of acquisition, distinct amounts of time spent abroad, and the type of interaction between learners and native speakers is not specified. The findings of my research are important in that they provide data relating development in certain linguistic elements and in oral communication skills to interaction and social networks during the study abroad experience.

The subsequent chapters of this book detail the acquisition of five learners in a semester-long experience in Buenos Aires, Argentina. The data reveal details about what can actually take place in the study abroad context. I first outline in Chapter 1 the theoretical framework by surveying theories on input, interaction, motivation, social networks, and acculturation. I then describe in Chapter 2 the research design I used with that theoretical framework in mind and I also introduce the reader to the learners who participated in the project. In Chapters 4 and 5, I discuss the quantitative (development seen in linguistic accuracy and oral communication skills) and qualitative data (significance of certain types of interaction in second language acquisition and the interdependence of the maintenance of social network interactions, attitudes, and motivation) leading the way to Chapter 5 that integrates the observations on the development in linguistic accuracy and oral communication skills with observations on individual factors.

Chapter 1
STUDY ABROAD AND THEORIES OF SECOND LANGUAGE ACQUISITION

While living in Argentina collecting data for this project, it was challenging for me to interact with my host family, maybe it was because I was an experienced study abroader that did not need to depend on my host family for survival strategies. Argentina, or better yet Buenos Aires, is a city where friends tend to know each other for a very long time, so the difficulty of interacting, not only with my host family (who had a same aged man in the house as I), but also with the culture was challenging. I must note that I did make some very good friends who migrated to Buenos Aires from Misiones, succeeding in creating my own social network while simultaneously observing the study abroad participants. In other words, it was not an ideal host culture. I had to make an effort to interact with the native speakers, travel and meet people to make new friends, and more importantly, acculturate myself into the environment. One can only imagine the difficulties that a first time study abroad learner has as s/he tries to interact within the new host culture, balancing the factors of language development and interaction in the host culture, which may have a positive or negative effect on her/his acquisition process. Numerous studies have shown the importance of interaction, acculturation, and environment in SLA, I briefly describe them in the following section.

Theories on Input and Interaction

Research on second language learners' speech has focused on the effects of input and interaction on second language acquisition. Hypotheses on input and interaction have been offered to account for various aspects of second language acquisition, specifically, comprehensible input, negotiating for meaning, attention, and scaffolding.

Pica (1987) states that research has revealed that second languages are not learned through memorization of their rules and structures, but through internalization of these rules from input that is made comprehensible within a context of social interaction. Gass and Selinker (1994, p. 219) summarize Long's (1981) Interaction Hypothesis, which comprises three premises: (1) comprehensible input is necessary for acquisition; (2) conversational interactions with negotiation makes the input comprehensible; and (3) comprehensible output aids learners in moving from semantic processing to syntactic processing. In Krashen's (1985) Monitor Model, one of five hypotheses he proposes is the Input Hypothesis used to explain how acquisition takes place. He posits that second language acquisition depends on modified, comprehensible input, as follows (p. 2):

> The Input Hypothesis claims that humans acquire language in only one way – by understanding messages, or by receiving 'comprehensible input.' We progress along the natural order by understanding input that contains structures at our next 'stage' – structures that are a bit beyond our current level of competence (We move from i, our current level, to $i+1$, the next level along the natural order by understanding input containing $i+1$).

That is, the learner understands input that contains grammatical forms that are a little more advanced than the current state of the learner's interlanguage. One critique of this hypothesis is that it does not specify how extralinguistic information aids in actual acquisition. As stated by Gass and Selinker (1994, p. 150), "We may be able to understand something that is beyond our grammatical knowledge, but how does that translate into grammatical acquisition?"

A notion in second language acquisition research that attempts to specify how extralinguistic information aids acquisition is that of negotiation. Gass and Varonis (1994, p. 299) show that negotiations are an integral part in interactive conditions especially when those negotiations focus the learner's attention on problematic input. The authors claim that:

> Interactional input provides a forum for learners to readily detect a discrepancy between their learner language and the target language and that awareness of the mismatch serves the function of triggering a modification of existing second language knowledge.

Attention allows learners to notice a disparity between what they know about the language and what native speakers produce. This mismatch or discrepancy is what Gass (1997, p. 4) refers to as "a gap in knowledge" and the perception of such a gap may lead to grammar restructuring. Dörnyei and Scott (1997) also refer to gaps in speakers' knowledge preventing them from verbalizing messages. They claim that this type of "resource deficit" may lead the learner to become aware of the communication problem and implement a communication "strategy" to negotiate meaning (p. 185).

According to Lightbown (1985), restructuring outside of the classroom acquisition context occurs due to the complex language system where "an increase in error rate in one area may reflect an increase in complexity or accuracy in another, followed by overgeneralization of a newly acquired structure" (p. 177). When additional syntactic patterns become available to learners, restructuring or destabilization occurs. According to Lightbown, destabilization is at the base of language change. Lantolf and Appel (1994) add to the literature on interaction as an integral part of acquisition by applying Vygotsky's (1978) theories of child learning to adult second language acquisition. Vygotsky explains a child's progression from a stage in which the facts of the environment control the child to one in which the child controls the activity. Vygotsky (1978, p. 86) labels this progression the Zone of Proximal Development (ZPD) and posits it as the site of learning. He defines the ZPD as:

> the distance between the actual development level as determined by independent problem solving and the level of potential development as

determined through problem solving under adult guidance or in collaboration with more capable peers.

In extending this framework from child to adult language learning, Lantolf and Appel (1994) highlight the process of voluntary acting that is distributed between two people, "the expert", who already knows how to perform a particular act, and "the novice", who does not. The authors state that the difference between what the novice is able to produce when acting alone and when producing language under the guidance of a more experienced language user is the manner in which more difficult topics are managed.

Donato's (1994) research on language learners also uses Vygotsky's (1978) ZPD as its theoretical framework to describe interaction and its role in second language acquisition. Donato claims that when learners are in a context where interaction occurs with a more expert speaker, they notice new or correct structures in the expert speaker's language or feedback. They are then able to use the new information to build on, or "scaffold," their developing interlanguage. Donato adds the notion of "scaffolding" to the previously discussed framework of Gass and Varonis (1994), in which attention allows learners to notice a mismatch between what they know about the language and what is produced by native speakers.

Theories on Motivation, Social Networks, and Acculturation

These next set of theories illustrate the value that interaction has on the developing interlanguage of a learner. It presents the concepts of comprehensible input, negotiation, attention to input, and scaffolding, which are significant to this study because I hypothesize that learners that are members of social networks in which interaction with native speakers occurs, will receive sufficient opportunities to notice gaps in their interlanguage and therefore will build their interlanguage to create a higher level of competence.

Schumann's (1976) study was one of the first to show that the environment in which the learners interact, the opportunities to use the language, and their attitudinal and motivational patterns, all seem to have a direct influence on the rate of acquisition. Milroy (1987) defines interactions of language use as "social networks," or the informal social relationships contracted by an individual. According to Milroy, analysis of these social networks can be used to account for variation between speakers at the level of the individual.

Information found in a theoretical article on social networks by Blom and Gumperz (1972) concerning the use of low- and high-status dialects of Norwegian can be applied somewhat to the study abroad learner. To describe their investigation briefly, they noted that the heaviest low-status dialect users in a first language Norwegian community generally were members of closed, or dense, networks. Milroy (1987) reasons that this pattern occurs because low-status speakers interact mostly within a defined territory and all the contacts know each other. On the other hand, the elite have open personal networks. They tend to move outside territorial boundaries and each person's contacts have their own contacts, none of which necessarily know each other.

Milroy (1987) extends Blom and Gumperz's (1972) conclusions regarding closed and open relationships between members of a community to account for variability in individual linguistic behavior in the community. Milroy (1987, p. 21) states that where networks are dense, role relationships are usually multiplex. In other words, the individuals interact with each other in more than one capacity. Milroy concludes that a dense and multiplex network structure has the capacity to impose linguistic norms upon its members. If a speaker's personal network is relatively loose-knit, it will not constitute a bounded group capable of enforcing a focused set of linguistic norms. Instead, it is more susceptible to the influence of a prestige norm.

This pattern of interacting outside "territorial boundaries" versus maintaining "closed or dense networks" can be related to study abroad learners who are acquiring a second language. I pose here an extension of Milroy (1987) and Blom and Gumperz's (1972) previously mentioned theories of social networks of people in their native communities to learners in a study abroad context, which provides the framework of social networks for this study.

Learners in the host country who do not interact with the host culture but instead form closed, multiplex networks with other English-speaking learners will interact mostly within this English-speaking territory. All their contacts will be with one another, making their role relationships multiplex, as can be seen in Figure 1.

Figure 1. High Density, Closed Personal Network Structure. (X is the focal point of the network) (Milroy, 1987, p. 20)

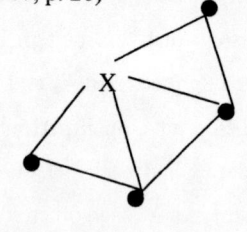

Each person X is viewed as a focus from which lines radiate to points (persons with whom X is in contact). In this dense network structure of English-speaking members, interaction will normally be in English; such interaction is, naturally, not conducive to acquiring Spanish. The learners who participate in this type of network structure limit their opportunities to interact with native speakers. They accordingly limit chances to notice new or correct structures in the native speakers' language or feedback, which limits the new information that can scaffold their already developing interlanguage. This dense, multiplex network structure with other study abroad learners will slow down the development of these learners' interlanguage toward a close approximation with the target language. The optimal situation is to have a dense, multiplex network structure with native Spanish speakers.

On the other hand, study abroad learners who have open personal networks, moving outside the first language English-speaking territory of their fellow study abroad acquaintances, will attain contacts in the host culture, presumably with native speakers. The open network tie is understandably uniplex since they have just arrived to a country where they have to build relationships within a new social network, usually starting with one member at a time. Even when the learner is housed with a family and seems to have easier access to a new social network, it does not preclude the fact that the relationships with the new members still have to be built.

Figure 2. Low Density, Open Personal Network Structure. (X is the focal point of the network) (Milroy, 1987, 20)

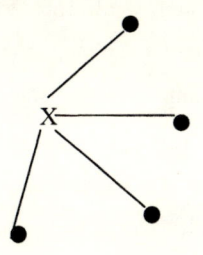

In this low density, open uniplex network, the learner X associates with native speakers (points) in a single capacity. In other words, the individual interacts with the others as just a neighbor or employee, rather than in multiple capacities such as friends may do. This open, personal network characterizes the network of a typical study abroad learner who maintains contact with several native speakers in a single context. This network is also the foundation in establishing an extension to a multiplex network. For example, when the uniplex interaction is that of only school colleagues, then interaction with the native typically deals with topics such as school, assignments, and tests. Within these conversations on a simple topic, over time, the learner can become an expert at talking about, for example, only school topics. The learner is infrequently exposed to topic variety that comes up in multiplex interactions where complex descriptions, arguments, and supporting of opinions occur. The learner then has to develop a wider range of oral ability functions to be able to communicate a point of view effectively in the second language and over a wide range of topics.

Although this uniplex network is the only type that learners can expect to establish when new to the country, this situation changes when the learners' social network extends to one of a more multiplex nature. Within a multiplex network, the interactions with native-speaker members help their interlanguage reach a close approximation with the second language faster. The learners in a multiplex network are required to speak to each member in various capacities, not only as a colleague but also perhaps as a friend. In this manner, the interactions would then include a wider range of topics that allow the learners to practice varying aspects of the second language with more frequency and to encounter opportunities to notice gaps which leads to scaffolding, allowing for the restructuring of their interlanguage.

"Network zones" are important to understanding the role that social networks play in successful interaction. The persons who are directly linked to X are characterized by Milroy (1987, p. 46) as "belonging to his [or her] *first order* network zone." Each of these people may be in contact with others whom X does not know, but with whom X could come into contact via the first order zone. These more distantly connected persons form X's "*second order* zone." Milroy discusses these zones to demonstrate to future fieldworkers why creating a link with the local networks is important in collecting reliable ethnographic data. I extend this framework to study abroad learners.

Figure 3. Low Density Network Showing First and Second Order Zones. (Milroy, 1987, p. 48)

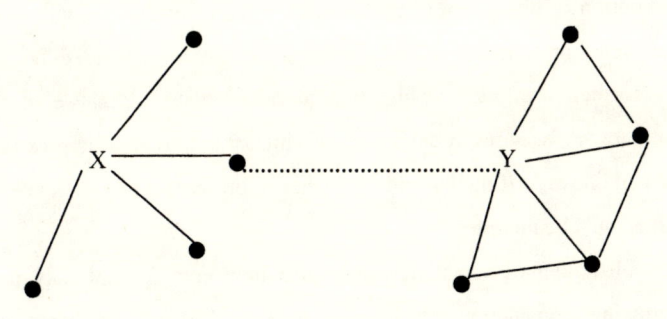

Low-density, open 1st order zone High-density, closed 2nd order zone

Messages that pass along these network links are seen as transactions, "governed by the principle that the value gained by an individual in a transaction is equal to, greater than, the cost" (p. 49). These transactions may consist of greetings, civilities, jokes, information, or assistance, and when they flow in both directions between links, they are considered "exchanges." When the learner X participates in a social network of which native-speaker Y is part of a second order zone that is closed, then:

> Friends of friends perform an important social function by extending the range of goods and services[1] which members of the first order zone are able to provide. Therefore, if a stranger is identified as a friend of a friend, he may easily be drawn into the network's mesh of exchange and obligation relationships. His chances of observing and participating in prolonged interaction will then be considerably increased (p. 53).

The learners in the networks with native speakers, as opposed to those in

---

[1] These goods and services may be material or may stem from qualities of personality or leadership.

the closed networks of other study abroad English-speaking learners, will acquire a set of linguistic norms that are enforced by exchange with those native-speaker contacts. The notion of obligation is contingent on that of exchange. Milroy (p. 49) states that sometimes more valued transactions may be provided by one person than the other, creating an obligation to return them. Because of this inequality, the network becomes a device upon which the individual is pressured to behave in a certain way. If the individual wishes to protect social relationships, these obligations must be honored.

The establishment of social networks in a new environment may be a difficult undertaking, considering that learners have to deal with elements of a host culture that they never had to deal with in their own country. The maintenance, however, of second order zone, closed social networks with native speakers of the host culture may be more difficult if the learner does not wish to or know how to foster the new social relationship. The negligence or care of social relationships by the learner is caused by many factors, but in the study abroad context, the learner's cultural awareness or acculturation plays an important role.

Schumann (1978, p. 160) states, "[T]he degree to which the learner acculturates to the target language group will control the degree to which he acquires the second language." Sociological research on acculturation identifies four stages of cultural adjustment that learners pass through while adapting to and learning about a new culture: (a) honeymoon stage; (b) culture shock; (c) culture stress; and (d) recovery. Bennett (1986) provides a more detailed model of acculturation, and while his model does not address second language learning, it does provide an appropriate characterization of the study abroad learner's experience. The model states that one must pass through a state of ethnocentrism in order to reach a state of ethnorelativism or acculturation. This progress from ethnocentrism to ethnorelativism occurs through a sequence of six states.

The first three states fall under the principle of ethnocentrism: (a) the learner denies the existence of cultural differences, which includes isolation and separation stages; (b) the reality of cultural differences is recognized but an effort is made to preserve hegemony of one culture over another; (c) cultural differences are minimized in an effort to deal with the recognition that it is not tenable to preserve the superiority of one culture over another.

The last three states fall in the category of ethnorelativism: (d) a state that is described by stages of behavior and value relativism in which the learner acknowledges the possibility of differences among cultures in adapting to the environment; (e) adaptation is made to the host culture, in which a sense of understanding and pluralism arise; and (f) a state is established in which differences in general become essential to identity (p. 27).

Citron (1995) proposes a hypothesis towards a theory of ethnolingual relativity that encompasses a central idea, stating that openness to contrasting cultural and linguistic patterns of other peoples and a refusal to be limited by one's own cultural and linguistic experiences can facilitate second language learning. He defines ethnolingual relativity as the ability to recognize that (a) languages are not direct translations of each other and (b) the way one's first language expresses a thought is arbitrary.

> For example, in the English sentence, "I like that joke," *I* am the subject of the sentence and am acting on my environment. When the Spanish language expresses the thought, "Me gusta ese chiste," it is the joke that is having its effect on me. The first sub-component of ethno-lingual relativity, then, is understanding that this same thought is expressed in different ways syntactically in each language and that neither way is more correct that the other (p. 106).

Citron goes on to state that "social attitude may be linked to ethnolingual relativity as learners without such an open perspective may be less motivated to learn a new language since it would seem less relevant to them" (p. 108). Since there is no known empirical documentation that supports these perceptions that cross cultural understanding could aid second language acquisition, Citron states that the ethnolingual relativity hypothesis would gain "significant support if research on students studying abroad were to show the gains in language skills corresponded to gains in cross cultural understanding" (p. 110).

It is important to understand that social networks correlate closely to how the learners envision themselves in the host culture. For example, Dowell (1995) noted that the learners in a study abroad program in Mexico "seemed to spend a considerable amount of time participating in activities reflecting their home culture rather than engaging in many traditional host-culture activities. When the latter occurred, it typically had a US American twist to it" (p. 6). One cannot expect that learners will be motivated to learn the target language and integrate themselves into the host culture if they find themselves in a state where segregation of the two cultures is still an integral part of their cultural outlook.

According to Gardner and Lambert (1959), an integrative motivation to learn the target language is linked to positive attitudes toward the target language group and the potential for integrating into that group or interacting with its members. In a later study, Gardner (1985) reveals that it is not the instrumental or integrative orientation that influences achievement, but rather the motivation. He identifies a distinction between orientations and motivations: orientations refer to reasons for studying a second language, whereas motivation refers to the directed, reinforcing effort to learn the language.

Research on learners abroad showing that gains in language skills correspond to gains in cross cultural understanding not only lends support to Citron's hypothesis of ethnolingual relativity, but documents the role of positive social attitudes towards the host culture in the second language acquisition process. This positive social attitude, together with the necessity that learners integrate themselves into the community to acquire the target language, emphasizes the importance of research that will reveal the stages that learners pass through during the acquisition process and whether they do, in fact, ever reach a state of "ethnorelativism" or "ethnolingual relativity" during the stay abroad.

The Role of Ethnographic Research

Since this study aims both to describe and to account for the regularities and the variations in the social behavior of language learners in the study abroad context I used ethnographic research to collect the data since it is a tool that helps to understand the human species with a goal to describe and explain the regularities and variations in social behavior. It is one task to describe the differences in learners, however, and another to account for them. Spradley (1979) identifies an important contribution of ethnographic research, that of informing culture bound theories. Each culture provides people with a way of seeing the world and defines the world in which people live. Culture includes assumptions about the nature of reality and includes values that specify what is good, true, and believable. Whenever people learn a new culture, they are "imprisoned," or culture bound, without knowing it. "Ethnography alone seeks to document the existence of *alternative* realities and to describe these realities in their own terms" (Spradley, 1979, p. 11).

Let us take, for example, the study abroad language learners' attitudinal variations toward the host culture. Data collected through ethnographic interviews and journals may reveal that some learners remain bound to their own culture while others are not. The qualitative analysis here looks at what learners said in their informal interviews and what they logged in their diaries to describe in what ways the learners remained culture bound and to account for the variability in their attitudes. Their written statements also reveal much about their motivation to form networks and learn Spanish, which may not be reflected in a simple questionnaire. Ethnography produces empirical data about the lives of the learners in specific situations.

Research Questions

The previously cited research address various aspects of SLA. At this time, however, there has been little work published that relates specifically to the effect of immersion on the acquisition of linguistic elements or how second language interaction with native speakers leads to acquisition gains in the study abroad context. This is where my research attempts to fill part of that gap and others concerning extralinguistic influences by addressing the following research questions:

1. What development is seen in the learners' linguistic accuracy in Spanish while abroad?

2. What degree of corresponding development of their oral communication skills can be noted?

3. What individual extralinguistic factors (such as motivation, contact with host culture outside of the classroom, and attitudes towards the host culture) can be related to development of skills and accuracy?

4. What is the minimal amount of time learners should spend abroad to benefit linguistically from the experience?

With the data collected to answer these four research questions, I shed light on several aspects of SLA in the study abroad context. First, I demonstrate that the extension of social networks in the host community correlate with the learners' development in both oral communication skills in Spanish and accuracy. Secondly, I demonstrate that the study abroad learners who possess a positive motivational orientation towards learning the language (be it integrative, instrumental, or intrinsic) will participate in interactions with the people of the host culture. Third, I establish a connection between learners' social attitudes toward the host culture and their motivational perseverance to learn the target language. Finally, I show that the time needed for each learner to benefit linguistically from the study abroad experience is related to the time necessary to form and maintain a social network.

Chapter 2
PARTICIPANTS AND THE DATA COLLECTION AND ANALYSIS PROCESS

Learner Participants

During the same time that the learner participants were filling out paperwork and being interviewed for the Argentina study abroad program in the Spring of 1997, I was making long-distance contacts with various professors and study abroad program coordinators in Buenos Aires, Argentina. I wanted to arrive to Buenos Aires and be able capture the participants' goals, preoccupations, and language abilities within the week they had arrived in order to get a true picture of their development when compared to the week before they had to leave. This meant that I needed the University's permission for me to have access to their North American study abroad students before I even stepped foot in Argentina. I was granted this permission by the Universidad del Salvador, which allowed me to do the fieldwork for this study over a six-month period (mid July to mid December 1997).

The participants, from whom the data were collected, were selected from a group of study abroad students that were part of a consortium among the University of Texas at Austin, the University of Illinois at Urbana-Champaign, and the University of North Carolina at Chapel Hill. I provide the following excerpt from an informational packet given to students before going abroad to give the reader an idea of the this consortium's program goals and what was expected of the students once abroad:

[T]o promote both integration and exposure to diverse sectors of Argentine society. Integration is achieved through enrollment in regular university courses so that you are forced to excel in the Spanish language, receive exposure to a different educational system, and have the opportunity to share academic and social interests with your Argentine peers. The second goal of diversity is fulfilled by the opportunity to take courses at three different universities.

The three universities were the Universidad de Buenos Aires (UBA), Universidad Torcuato di Tella (UTDT), and Universidad del Salvador (USAL). The students were able to enroll in courses at all three institutions or just one, based on their interest in the classes offered at that time. Although UBA is a public university, UTDT is a private university, and USAL is a private Catholic university, I discovered through contact with the students that this difference did not influence them to take courses at any one university. The consortium liaison in Buenos Aires provided me with a list of the students' phone numbers and I proceeded to call only those who were taking classes at USAL since permission for the study was granted from that university.

Eleven students were contacted by phone and passed the initial interview to find out if they spoke or had studied another foreign language prior to their study abroad. At a subsequent meeting, the students were told more about the project and the conditions of participation: to fill out weekly network logs, keep a weekly diary, consent to being recorded five times, and take an oral pre- and post-program oral proficiency test. The learners were informed that no evaluation or correction of their language abilities would be made during the data collection process.

The initial eleven students agreed to fill out a questionnaire which were evaluated and seven students were selected on the basis of the following criteria outlined by Huebner (1995): (a) willingness to participate in the project (Appendix A); (b) a pre-program simulated oral proficiency interview (SOPI) level of Intermediate, according to the ACTFL Proficiency Guidelines (2000); (c) background factors such as foreign language and cultural background (i.e., those who had traveled extensively abroad or had studied or spoke any language other than English were disqualified); (d) motivation to learn Spanish, as indicated by their concrete plans to continue studying Spanish after the semester in Argentina and their desire to learn Spanish for reasons other than to meet course, major, or degree requirements; and (e) realistic expectations of program outcome. The participants' only study abroad experience was the semester of study in Buenos Aires.

At USAL, the informants attended a biweekly language class for international students that was taught exclusively in Spanish. In addition to this multi-nationally populated language class, the participants also attended courses in areas such as Agriculture, Economics, International Business, and Politics. The study abroad students were expected to produce the same quality papers and projects as the Argentine students in the classes.

The participants ranged in age from 19 to 21 years old, with an average age of 19.9 years, and their ethnicity was Caucasian. Of the original six women and the five men, six discontinued participation after several months into the project. Gender did not enter into the selection process of the participants, and the greater number of males than females was purely coincidental. Thus, five participants served as the informants for this study. They were from diverse regions of the US, from both rural and urban cities, and were eager to volunteer as participants in this study.

Stan[2] was a 20-year-old senior undergraduate student who was pursuing a major in Latin American business at a large private school on the East Coast. Prior to the 1997 fall session in Buenos Aires, he had studied Spanish for four semesters in college and had traveled in Brazil. Stan was a conscientious and serious student who was more interested in the politics and culture of Argentina than in partying. His expectations of the study abroad program were to travel,

---

[2]Names of the participants have been changed to protect their anonymity.

learn Spanish, and understand the culture. Stan planned to use his Spanish in the US and possibly live in a Spanish-speaking country after graduation.

Tom was a 21-year-old senior at a small state college in the Southeast. Tom was an outgoing and eager student who was willing to try anything and everything. Within a month of his stay in Argentina he already had his favorite ice-cream locale and knew the words to popular Argentine rock music. Prior to the 1997 fall session in Buenos Aires, he had studied Spanish for four years in secondary school and four semesters in college. Tom's reason for learning Spanish was that he wanted to work overseas in the future. His expectations of the program were to return to the US with a strong grasp of the language and confidence in his speaking. He planned to implement Spanish in his work and to socialize with Spanish-speaking people.

Mark was a 19-year-old junior at a large state university in the West. Mark also had a very good-natured, easy-going, and open personality and was very sociable. His evenings usually consisted of partying with other students and natives. It was effortless to carry out ethnographic interviews with Mark because he usually volunteered much personal information. Prior to the 1997 fall session in Buenos Aires, he had studied Spanish for two years in high school and four semesters in college. Mark hoped that knowing Spanish would distinguish him from other people in the job world. His expectations of the study abroad program were to achieve near fluency in the language and gain a unique perspective from inside another culture. He planned to join the Foreign Service or at least be able to use his Spanish with whatever job he might obtain in his home state.

Sam, 21 years old, was a senior at a large state university in the Northwest. Sam was a quiet person who always seemed to have an Argentine newspaper in his house. He usually kept to himself but he did frequent the local bars and attend study abroad students' parties. Prior to the 1997 fall session in Buenos Aires, he had studied Spanish for two years in high school and two and a half years in college. Sam wanted to learn Spanish since he believed it is one of the most important languages in the US and in the world. His expectations were to make great improvements in his ability to speak Spanish and he planned to spend time in both Mexico and Spain within the next couple of years.

Jennifer was a 19-year-old third-year undergraduate student at a large state university in the Midwest. She was a good-natured, shy person who enjoyed exercising and spending time with children. Interviewing Jennifer was somewhat difficult since she only reluctantly volunteered information about her experiences in Argentina and her quantity of speech, spoken in a soft voice, was usually at a minimum. Her expectations of the study abroad program were to become competent in the language in order to benefit her in her future line of work in agriculture. Prior to the 1997 fall session in Buenos Aires, she had studied Spanish for four semesters in college.

One student lived with a host family and four lived in student apartments with between one and three roommates from different parts of the world. Those who did have English-speaking roommates had a rule to communicate with each other only in Spanish. At the time of the fieldwork, two informants taught conversational English in small language schools as a source for income.

Data Collection Instruments

The simulated oral proficiency interview

The quantitative measurements for this study were derived from a Simulated Oral Proficiency Interview (SOPI) and five informal interviews. The sole purpose of the SOPI was to have quantitative data on pre- and post-program oral proficiency[3] performance with a controlled measurement.

---

[3] Oral proficiency is used in this study to refer specifically to an evaluation of target language use reflected in the Oral Proficiency Interview (OPI) score. Oral fluency refers to those aspects of oral ability having to do with the fluidity or "smoothness" of language use (Freed, 1995b; Freed, Segalowitz, & Dewey, 2004; Segalowitz & Freed, 2004).

The SOPI is a performance-based speaking test that emulates the speaking section of the ACTFL Proficiency Interview (Breiner-Sanders, et al., 2000). This instrument tests the speaking abilities of speakers to assess their proficiency in a second language. The SOPI was chosen as a means to assess oral ability since I was most familiar with the test format and criteria for grading and believed it would yield a reliable indication of growth of oral ability. The prototypical SOPI, developed by the Center for Applied Linguistics, consists of several parts used to elicit different speech functions. The interview used here was a sample SOPI prepared by the Center for Applied Linguistics for the state of Texas, the Texas Oral Proficiency Test, which is used to certify prospective elementary and high school Spanish and bilingual educators for language competency. The SOPI was chosen to document changes in the participants' oral ability while abroad because the SOPI "has shown itself to be a valid and reliable surrogate of the OPI" (Stansfield, 1990, p. 229) (see Clark & Li, 1986; Shohamy, Gordon, Kenyon, & Stansfield, 1989; Stansfield, Kenyon, Paiva, Doyle, Ulsh, & Cowles, 1990)[4]. It was given as a pre- and post-program test by me, a trained SOPI rater, and the learners' proficiency was scored using a modified version of the ACTFL Proficiency Guidelines scale.

The SOPI were carried out in the participants' homes at times convenient to them. The SOPI was administered following procedures regarding instructions and time limits. One difference between the SOPI used in this study and the official SOPI is that I, and not a recorded message, prompted the students to speak. This human aspect of the proficiency test allowed for a more natural interview to take place, as opposed to a test carried out by means of a tape

---

[4]As cited in Freed (1995b, p. 143), "Despite the fact that the OPI is now widely used as a measurement instrument, it has been severely criticized on many grounds. Both Lennon (1990a, p. 397) and Olynyk, d'Angelijan, & Sankoff (1990, p. 153) criticize data elicited through oral interviews, suggesting that the speech obtained in this way is indicative of a student's least fluent variety of interlanguage."

recorder without human presence, as is normally done with the SOPI.

Stansfield and Kenyon's (1996) update on the SOPI describes that the test begins with personal background questions. During a brief pause, the examinee records a short answer to each question. The rest of the test contains performance-based tasks designed to elicit specific language functions. These tasks assess the examinee's ability to perform the various functions that characterize the Intermediate, Advanced, and Superior levels of the ACTFL Proficiency Guidelines (Breiner-Sanders, et al., 2000). Picture-based tasks require examinees to demonstrate the ability to give directions to someone using a map, describe a particular place based on a drawing, and narrate a sequence of events in the present, past, or future using drawings in the test booklet as a guide. Other tasks require examinees to speak on selected topics in which they demonstrate their ability to handle the functions and content that characterize the higher levels of proficiency according to the ACTFL Guidelines. These speaking functions include stating advantages and disadvantages, supporting an opinion, apologizing, and giving an informal talk.

I gave directions to all tasks presented in the test booklet in English. These directions contained a description of the context of the speaking task, including who the examinee would address, what the situation was, why the speaking task needed to be performed, and any other relevant information that made the task as authentic as possible. After reading and hearing these directions, examinees were given a brief pause to organize their thoughts. Next, I made a statement or asked a question in Spanish appropriate to the situation described in the English directions. The examinee attempted to perform the indicated task by responding with a reply that was appropriate for the situation. This format was repeated until the test was completed.

The informal interviews

In addition to the SOPI, I developed an informal interview protocol (Appendix B) to create a speech corpus to be analyzed for specific oral communication skills and linguistic accuracy. In these interviews, the five learners were asked the same open-ended questions. The informal interviews were not timed and the learners had some control of conversation topics. The prompt questions included greetings, leading questions designed to persuade the participants to perform some of the functions found in the SOPI, such as narrate personal experiences, express and support opinions, relate past activities, and tell future plans.

These informal interviews were added as a data collection tool in order to have month-to-month information to be able to chart the participants' oral language development. The SOPI was chosen to be used only as a pre- and post-test, instead of a for month-to-month measurement, so that the outcome of the SOPI would not be affected by practicing the same format on a monthly basis. The interviews were conducted exclusively in Spanish and the oral nature of the informal interviews helped to create an informal and natural setting. These interviews, which were recorded on an audiocassette recorder for about 15 minutes, were conducted once a month, for a total of five times.

Diary entries and network contact logs

Another especially important aspect for assessing development of oral ability abroad are tasks that help identify the environments, activities, and sociocultural views that lend themselves to be more or less successful for language acquisition. Accordingly, the qualitative data for this study were derived from diary entries and network contact logs. The results of the SOPI along with the narrative and ethnographic data give information with which to answer the third research question: What individual factors, such as social networks and attitudes towards a host culture, enter into successful second language development?

One means by which learners can record their thoughts, feelings, achievements, problems, strategies, and impressions of the culture is through diaries (Bacon, 1995; Oxford & Crookall, 1989). To this end, the participants were given notebooks in which they kept their weekly diary entries. They then turned in their diaries to me once a month to prevent any neglect in carrying out the task. The diary entries were written in English so that no subject material would be avoided due to limited linguistic capabilities in Spanish. Writing in English also allowed the participants to express themselves in as much detail as they desired.

Following Dowell's (1995) diary-writing guidelines, the participants were asked to use a variety of observations. The students usually wrote between 150 and 200 words per entry and were instructed to make comments on their perception of language progress, relay positive or negative events that had occurred within that week, give opinions, and make comparisons between US and Argentine traditions, food, transportation systems, education systems, and friendships.

After interviewing the participants and collecting the network logs and weekly diary entries, I then identified the learners' social networks in their study abroad environment. The establishment of uniplex networks and its development to multiplex, closed social networks in a new environment cannot be accomplished without advancement of the students' cultural understanding and acceptance (Bennett, 1986). The social network concept is used here as an illustrative device for describing social relations abroad from which one can learn how the learner participants envision and incorporate themselves in the host culture. These networks show how the learners are locating themselves in their new environment and, more importantly, they show the network of acquaintances, possibly predicting advancement in second language acquisition.

Data Analyses

I collected data for this study using four instruments to attempt to present a true picture of what takes place during the study abroad semester: pre- and post-program SOPIs, informal oral interviews, diaries, and social network contact logs. With the vast amount of information that was collected, I outline here the analyses that were performed with this data.

Simulated oral proficiency interview

SOPIs were scored to determine the pre- and post-program oral proficiency ratings of the five participants. The SOPIs were double-rated for reliability and, if a discrepancy was found between the two ratings, a third, and different rater was used. Following a modified version of the ACTFL Proficiency Guidelines (Breiner-Sanders, et al., 2000), the SOPIs were rated according to the criteria described for the following four levels: Intermediate Low, Intermediate Mid, Intermediate High, and Advanced.[5] The levels adhere to the definitions presented by Byrnes and Canale (1987, pp. 16-17).

To contrast the top two categories examined here, an Intermediate High speaker is characterized as having emerging evidence of connected discourse, particularly for simple narration and description, but errors are evident. The Advanced speaker, in contrast, can narrate and describe with some detail and has the ability to handle past, present, and future verbs well, and makes few agreement errors. Characteristics of a more experienced speaker of a language include high linguistic accuracy, the ability to state and support opinions and to give detailed descriptions instead of identifying discrete elements, and to tell a story instead of listing occurrences.

---

[5] The other ACTFL proficiency levels outlined by Breiner-Sanders, et al. (2000) -- Novice Low, Novice Mid, Novice High, Advanced Plus, and Superior -- were not applicable to the learners in this study.

Informal oral interviews

There are many features of the learners' language that can be analyzed longitudinally to show development in oral ability. Chapter 3 of this study focuses on two elements of the informal oral interviews: linguistic accuracy and function. Function refers to what the user does with the language, or the user's oral communication skills. Function is assessed here by checking for use and degree of elaboration of descriptions and narrations, and supporting opinions. These elements, with the exception of opinions, were selected as being of special interest because they vary in definition depending on whether the speaker is at an Intermediate or Advanced level. For example, the Intermediate speaker produces descriptions and some narration with discrete sentences and minimal information whereas the Advanced speaker produces paragraph-length descriptions and narrations. Sustained production of opinions and supporting arguments appears only at the Advanced High and Superior levels.

Classification of data: Linguistic accuracy

The learners' informal interviews were transcribed and analyzed for: (a) tense selection of present vs. past; (b) imperfect vs. preterite aspect selection; (c) person-number (subject-verb) agreement; and (d) gender-number agreement. I limit the focus to these syntactic elements since any considerable number of errors in (a) and (b) could hinder comprehensibility (although errors in other elements such as lexicon could also hinder comprehensibility). Errors in (c) and (d) were targeted because accuracy in agreement is an element that shows improvement over time in language learners. These syntactic elements were also focused on since the SOPI guidelines list confusion of aspect and tense selection and agreement errors as markers of distinct oral proficiency levels. The above-mentioned categories were placed in chart form and a tally mark was made for inappropriate use.

As similarly noted in Collentine's (2004) study, I realize that this broad analysis will examine accuracy in these structures in both marked and unmarked contexts, which may lead to an expected higher score on all these features during the experiment.[6] I am also aware that there are two categories of (d), gender-number agreement. The first category includes both the subject predicate agreement (Soy profesora 'I am a professor [feminine]') and the nominal predicate agreement (Estoy contento/a 'I am happy [masculine/feminine]'). The second type of gender-number agreement is found within noun phrases, as seen in example (2.3). In the analysis, I made no differentiation between agreement errors and I included all agreement errors together within the subject and nominal predicate categories and noun phrases. Examples of inappropriate use are seen in (2.1) to (2.4):

(2.1) [In response to ¿Tienes cuentos que me puedes decir? 'Do you have any stories that you can tell me?'] Este[7] semana pasada uh mi familia tenía tres cumpleaños en una semana, y oof muy loco. Y la abuela uh...visitó su, nuestra casa. Y uh, y **tenemos**[present] para cada cumpleaños una festeja.

This last week uh my family had three birthdays in one week, and oof very crazy. And the grandmother uh...visited her, our house. And uh, and we have a party for each birthday.

The verb tenemos in (2.1) is well formed even though it is expressed in the present, rather than the target past tense tuvimos.

(2.2) [In response to ¿Qué hiciste en Salta? 'What did you do in Salta?'] Fuimos...encima de el cerro de la ciudad uh...**hubo**[preterite]...muchas tiendas en...una plaza bella.

---

[6]According to Collentine (2004, footnote), "Lafford and Collentine (1989) demonstrated that, in conversational discourse, second-language learners of Spanish produce many unmarked grammatical forms and few marked grammatical forms. This presents a dilemma for the second language researcher, since accuracy measurements that consider both the marked and unmarked forms of a paradigm most likely inflate the actual expertise that a learner has with any given structure."

[7]Corrections for spelling and grammar are not made by the author in the learners' excerpts.

We went...on top of the hill of the city uh...there were[preterite]*...many stores in...a beautiful plaza.*

In (2.2), the verb <u>hubo</u> is well formed even though it is expressed in the preterite, rather than the target imperfect aspect <u>había.</u>

> (2.3) ...**las personas**[3rd person plural] de la oficina de intercambio me **despertó**[3rd person singular] esta mañana...
>
> ...*the people*[plural] *in the student exchange office woke*[singular] *me up this morning...*

The verb selection in (2.3) is correct even though the form is inappropriate in context: <u>las personas...despertó</u> shows the correct tense but lacks correct person-number agreement; the target here is <u>las personas...despertaron.</u>

> (2.4) ...hablamos sobre **los**[masculine, plural] **clases**[feminine, plural]...
>
> ...*we talked about the classes...*

Although the highlighted determinant and noun in (2.4), <u>los clases</u>, agree in number, the gender agreement is incorrect; the target here is <u>las clases</u>.

The linguistic elements were tallied as accurate or inaccurate, with no partial credit given. The reliability of the identification and classification of errors in the data is based on the experience that I have with the Spanish language through teaching and studying. The tally marks were then totaled for each category and divided by the total frequency of occurrences of that specific grammatical category in the speech sample to derive a percentage for grammatical accuracy. The procedure was repeated each month for the five months for each learner and results are presented in Chapter 3.

Classification of data: Oral communication skills

The informal interviews were transcribed, checked twice for accuracy, and were then analyzed according to the following procedure. Narrative passages were first identified within the dialogue between the participant and the interviewer. They were then categorized and tallied respectively by the type of function as listed by Galloway (1987), where the guidelines and implementations for the ACTFL Oral Proficiency Interview are defined.

The speaking guidelines comprise three sections, each with its own details: Context and Content, Function, and Accuracy. For the purpose of this study, focus was placed on only Function and Accuracy. Instead of using Galloway's (1987) analysis of Accuracy, I used the analysis outlined by the ACTFL Guidelines (1986), which I outlined in the previous section "Classification of data: Linguistic accuracy". The definition of Function was implemented to classify oral communication skills.

According to Galloway (1987, p. 30), Function "is perhaps the most crucial element in oral proficiency assessment. If the speaker cannot combine linguistic resources to perform communicative tasks, explicit knowledge of grammar and vocabulary is of questionable value." The continuum that Galloway claims as an indicator of developing proficiency includes three functions. It is considered that development has occurred in the functions of narrating in the past, giving descriptions, and supporting an opinion when the learner moves from: (1) listing occurrences to telling a story, meshing the descriptive background with the sequential recounting of events; (2) identifying discrete elements to providing the sensorial richness and explicitness of description; and (3) stating a simple opinion to providing cohesive and coherent arguments in support of that opinion. These lengthy descriptions are summarized in the following three Function categories: (1a) simple narration (Report); (1b) detailed narration (Story); (2a) simple description; (2b) detailed description; (3a) giving an opinion; and (3b) supporting an opinion. These Function categories are detailed with examples in the following sections.

Narration: Simple and Detailed Simple Narration has also been labeled as "Report" in past studies. Based on Polanyi's (1982, p. 515) definition, a Report tells only what happened "and may give some contextualizing information as well, setting the actions in a location and describing who was involved with their occurrence...[giving] a picture of what went on during a particular period" without explaining "why those events took place and why they are considered to be worth reporting" as in a story. Polanyi (1995) further describes that "a report will often have a flat or almost flat evaluation structure. Each proposition will be described in a rhetorically similar manner" (p. 276). The participant in (2.5) listed where she went, with whom she traveled, and how long the trip took.

(2.5) Simple Narration

    I: ¿Fuiste de vacaciones? [...]
    P: Sí. Yo fui a Iguazú y...también...fuimos a un...pueblo de Paraguay y...unas ruinas de una iglesia en...la provincia de Misiones. Yo fui con Elsa, Manuel, Fred y Gabriela. Y había un viaje en, era dieciocho horas en el colectivo.

    I: Did you go on vacation?[...]
    P: Yes. I went to Iguazú and...also...we went to a...town in Paraguay and...some church ruins in...the province of Misiones. I went with Elsa, Manuel, Fred, and Gabriela. And there was a trip in, it was eighteen hours in a bus.

This narrative passage, which occurred during the fifth month, was classified as Simple Narration since it tells what happened with minimal information and does not include descriptive background information that explains why it took place.

The following narrative in (2.6) occurred in the second month and was classified as a Detailed Narration, or Story. It was considered a definite past time narrative that the learner evaluated in such a way that the story recipients understood the "point" in telling the story. According to Polanyi (1982, p. 516), a story is told "to make a point, to transmit a message, often with some sort of moral about the world which one shares with the other people present." Evaluation[8] occurs in Stories; that is, the learner:

---

[8] See Polanyi (1989) for a more detailed discussion of "evaluation."

Includes meta-information throughout his telling of the story, which indicates the differential weight he assigns to the various states and events in the story. Some information thus emerges as more salient than others; with regard to the message the speaker is trying to convey (Polanyi, 1982, p. 516).

In excerpt (2.6), a participant tells a story to the interviewer in order to make a point that some immigrants in the US cannot always be believed. The first part of the excerpt is told to set up the story.

(2.6) Detailed Narration

[...] Yo le dije [to his French roommate], hay racismo, hay problemas pero no es tan grande, no es como vos, vos crees. Porque yo tengo que, vos tenés tu derecho de uh cree lo que vos querés pero yo tengo que decir como, porque yo vive, yo vivo en los Estados Unidos. No es tan malo como vos pensás. Y él [his French roommate] uh, él leyó un artículo sobre la, el haitian que los, la policía uh en Nueva York yo creo, ellos uh, uh golpearon y [...] y ellos "sodomized"...esto es lo que el haitian está diciendo. [...] Primero, vos no sabés si esto es la verdad porque, porque uh es posible que el hatian es, esto pasó, o es posible que él está diciendo mentiras porque él quiere dinero de la, de la ciudad o algo así. Y por eso tenés que leer con cuidado, no es posible leer todos los cosas y creen en todos los cosas. Tenés que leer bien. [...] Porque en Florida [...] yo trabajo [...] en los departamentos de muchos haitians y, yo oí cuentos de mi cuñado y el vecino de mi cuñado de haitians que siempre están en los coches y EERrr, ellos pararon muy rápido para [ ] el coche [slaps hands together] después o atrás para uh, hace un uh accidente. Y ellos reciben dinero or un, alguna vez el vecino de mi cuñado, es un uh bombero, y ellos llegaron a un accidente y habían cuatro haitians en el coche sin un uh sin un problema con el coche, no, pero el coche atrás había pe, pegado or al coche y por eso ellos no, no cambiaron la posición, "¡Oh, yo, no, no puedo muver, no puedo muver!" [...] y no había nada malo con el coche, el coche perfectamente. Por eso, no fue posible que el coche atrás pegó muy, muy rápido y por eso ellos tienen, los bomberos tienen que usar uh *the Jaws of Life*...Y ellos destruyeron, destruyeron todo el coche para uh muver la gente porque "oh, oh." Y todo esos cosas.

I told him [his French roommate], there is racism, there are problems but it is not as big, it is not like you think. Because I have to, you have your right to believe what you want but I have to say how because I live in the US It is not as bad as you think. And he [his French roommate] read an article about the Haitian that the police in New York I think, they uh, uh hit and [...] they sodomized...this is what the Haitian is saying. [...] First, you do not know if this is true because, because it is possible that the Haitian is, if this happened, or it is possible that he is telling lies because he wants money from the, from the city or something like that. And that is why you have to read carefully, it is not possible to read everything and believe in everything. You have to read carefully. [...] Because in Florida [...] I work [...] in the apartments of many Haitians and, I heard stories from my brother-in-law and my brother-in-law's neighbor about Haitians that always are in the cars and EERrrr, they stopped very fast for [ ] the car [slaps hands together] after or behind to uh, make an uh accident. And they receive money or an, one time my brother-in-law's neighbor, he's a uh firefighter, and they arrived at an accident and there were four Haitians in the car without an uh without a problem with the car, no, but the car behind had stu, struck or the car and so they didn't, didn't change the position. "Oh, I, can't, I can't move, I can't move" [...] and there wasn't anything wrong with the car, the car perfectly. And so, it wasn't possible that the car behind struck very, very fast and so they have, the firefighters have to use uh the Jaws of Life...And they destroyed, destroyed the entire car to uh move the people because "oh oh." And all those things.

This sample was considered a Detailed Narration, or Story, since the participant was trying to make the point of why he thought it was important to know the whole story behind a situation before drawing any conclusions. In this case, the learner was upset that his French roommate had made a generalization concerning American racism based on a separate incident involving a Haitian. In excerpt (3.4.2), he tells a story in which he tries to make the point that sometimes people lie to make situations look worse that they really are and conveys the message that this incident irritated him, a trait that is found in Storytelling (Liskin-Gasparro, 1993).

Description: Simple and Detailed Descriptions in this study are non-story narratives, which include: "plans, the simultaneous reporting of what is happening in an on-going situation, and descriptions of wished-for but not yet realized occurrences" (Polanyi, 1982, p. 511). A narrative passage that exemplifies the function of Simple Description, found during the fifth month in which another participant described to the interviewer her plans for the following week, is seen in (2.7):

(2.7) Simple Description

> I: Es nuestra última entrevista y...quiero saber lo que vas a hacer después...de esa semana.
> P: Bueno. Ya te digo que um jueves mis padres vienen y vamos a un viaje al sur en...Península Valdes. Vamos a alquilar un auto y, y ir para ver uh ballenas y ¿pingüinos?
> I: Pingüinos.
> P: Pingüinos, y...después um cuando revolvemos a Buenos Aires, Jackie y yo um nos vamos a un viaje al...uh...muchos partes de Sud América y [laughs] el quince de diciembre, me voy a Colorado.
>
> *I: It is our last interview and...uh I want to know what you are going to do after...this week.*
> *P: I already tell you that um Thursday my parents are coming and we are going on a trip to the south in...the Valdes Peninsula. We are going to rent a car, and are going to see um whales and, penguins?*
> *I: Penguins.*
> *P: Penguins, and...after when we return to Buenos Aires, Jackie and I are going on a trip to...many parts of South Am. and [laughs] the fifteenth of December, I am going to Colorado.*

It is clear here that the participant described to me her plans to travel outside of Buenos Aires by providing discrete elements about her trip. This excerpt was classified as a Simple Description because she did not provide any elaboration about her plans. On the other hand, when there is elaboration and explicitness of description, the narrative is classified as a Detailed Description function. An example can be seen in (2.8) from the fourth month in which a participant explains his opinion of study abroad.

(2.8) Detailed Description

> [...] Entonces, ah no sé...porque...porque todo el mundo que hace intercambio...siempre es como, "Sí, es una experiencia buenísimo," pero no aprendí nada de, de los cursos y...estas cosas. Pero está bien, es sólo un semestre. Bueno, estoy feliz que no quedo en esta situación por un

semestre más. No me gustaría uh ir a Salvador por más tiempo. Estoy harto, estoy harto con la universidad. Pero, me gustaría hacer una práctica como los franceses hacen acá...después de un semestre de estudios. Pero es, no sé, cómo uh cómo puedo hacerlo. Pero quiero, quiero terminar mis...estudios ahora con mis amigos, quiero graduarme con mis amigos. Por eso, por eso yo quiero, quiero volver para, para estar en, con todo. Y también, bueno, si yo quedo un semestre más, tengo que hacer más de cuatro años en la universidad. Y no quiero hacer más de cuatro años en la universidad.

[...] so, uh I don't know...because...because everyone that goes abroad...is always like, "Yes, it's an extremely good experience," but I didn't learn anything from, from the classes and...these things. But it's ok, it is just one semester. Well, I am happy that I am not staying in this situation for another semester. I wouldn't like to uh attend Salvador for a longer time. I am fed up, am fed up with that college. But, I would like to do an internship like the French do here...after one semester of studies. But it's, I don't know, how uh how I can do it. But I want, I want to finish my...studies now with my friends, I want to graduate with my friends. Therefore, therefore I want, I want to return to, to be in, with everything. And also, well, if I stay another semester, I have to do more than four years of college. I don't want to do more than four years of college.

Opinions: Giving and Supporting Another important function is that of Stating an Opinion. An Intermediate speaker has a tendency simply to state an opinion whereas the Advanced speaker provides cohesive and coherent arguments in support of that opinion. Consider the following excerpt from the third month in which an Intermediate participant explains his experience with the hospital system in Buenos Aires while he was sick.

(2.9) Giving an Opinion
  I: Y, ¿por qué te recomendaron ir a un hospital...privado?
  P: No, no sé, fui con Constanza de la oficina de OPII. Yo, dije que, "Puedo ir solo" y ella, ella está como, "Yo puedo ir contigo". Por eso, y, creo que es mucho mejor para ir al privada...Porque si no, voy a esperar mucho en, porque creo que hay mucha gente en la hospital local.

> I: And why did they recommend you go to a...private hospital...?
> P: I don't know, I went with Constanza of the OPII office. I, I said that, "I can go alone" and she, she is like, "I can go with you." So, and, I think that it is much better to go to the private one... Because if not, I am going to wait a lot in, because I think that there is a lot of people in the local hospital.

In this excerpt, he states that it is much better to go to a private hospital but gives no supporting arguments in support of that opinion. On the other hand, in the following excerpt, we can see an example of an Advanced Opinion with supporting arguments when a different explains to me that the university system in Buenos Aires is different from that of the US.

(2.10) Supporting an Opinion

> I: ¿Es diferente?
> P: Es demasiado diferente...los profesores no hablan de, de cosas que...yo no sé. Por ejemplo, yo fui a una clase, se llama..."Teoría de relaciones internacionales" y, clase de tres horas y por tres horas el profesor habla de todos los cosas además de relaciones internacionales y cosas como uh Primero Guerra Mundial y todos de esas cosas...que ya sé...Y, y los profesores no...va a las clases...muchos veces...No sé, la mayoría del tiempo no puedo entender el profesor so no, no hace falta [laughs]. So, a mí es...dificil pero...cuando realeza qué el profesor dijo uh...yo aprendo que la clase es...fácil. [laughs]

> I: Is it different?
> P: It is too different...the professors don't speak about, about things that...I don't know. For example, I went to a class, it's called... "Theory of Foreign Relations" and, three hour class and for three hours the professor speaks about everything besides international relations and things like uh First World War and all those things that...I already know...And, and the professors don't...go to the classes...many times...I don't know, the majority of the time I can't understand the professor so no, it's not necessary [laughs]. So, for me it is...difficult but...when I realize what the professor said uh...I learn that the class is...easy. [laughs]

The participant states his opinion that the school is very different from those in the US and provides three arguments to support his opinion: first, the professors talk about topics that have nothing to do with the course; second, many times the professors do not go to class; and finally, the class is easy.

In addition to classifying the narrative passages into the previously mentioned six functional categories (Simple and Detailed Description, Simple and Detailed Narration, and Giving and Supporting an Opinion), I used the appearance of the functions to mark instances of when the learner performed at a SOPI proficiency level. I do not attempt to infer an overall SOPI level via the informal interviews; rather, I use the markers to indicate when, during the stay abroad, the learner attempted more difficult functions.

Fluency The term "fluency" is not that easily defined and it is not the purpose of the study to attempt that feat (see Freed, 1995b; Freed, Segalowitz, & Dewey, 2004; Segalowitz & Freed, 2004 for a rather thorough discussion on fluency) but rather to use the factors mentioned in Freed's (1995b) study and also with the definition put forth by the scoring criteria of the ACTFL Proficiency Guidelines (1986) and measure the participants' development according to these elements. Therefore, the factors of fluency selected for analysis, from here on out marked as Fluency, were similar to both ACTFL's definition of "flow" of speech and Freed's (1995b), which were "primarily temporal features of speech and a variety of dysfluency markers which had emerged in prior studies as most salient in characterizing different levels of fluency in nonnative speakers (Ejzenberg, 1992; Lennon, 1990b; Olynyk, d'Angelijan, & Sankoff, 1990; Riggenback, 1989; Temple, 1992)" (pp. 129-130). These include:

1. Quantity of speech: calculated as raw frequencies of (non-repeated) words of the learners' responses to the interviewer's questions. Self repairs and repeats. Instances where learners repeat words or phrases in their attempt to create an understandable and cohesive discourse (Lafford, 1995, p. 109) were not tallied.

2. Flow of speech: the number of times the learner hesitated[9] with unfilled and filled pauses: calculated by counting silences which sounded dysfluent and also counting non-lexical fillers (i.e. uh and um) per response. In previous studies, dysfluent sounding silences tended to be of 400ms or more (Freed, 1995b; Freed, Segalowitz, & Dewey, 2004). Although I did not measure the pauses to verify if they were .4 seconds or longer, my experience as trained SOPI rater did give me a good "ear" measure for dysfluent hesitations.[10]

3. Number of times the learner struggled with the language: tallied and averaged per interview. One of the criterion set forth by Dörnyei and Scott (1997) was used to consider if learners were struggling with the language, specifically "own performance problems" in which they came to "the realization that something one has said is incorrect if only partly correct" (p. 183) which was associated with: (a) self-repair, self-rephrasing and self-editing mechanisms (Y me diga, le digo a él 'And he tells me, I tell him'); in addition to Lafford's (1995) strategy in which the learner requests feedback from the interviewer which was associated with (b) "confirmation checks" and "confirmation requests" (p. 117) (durmimos afuera la hosteria esta noche porque uh hubo una...curfew, no sé, ¿cómo se dice? 'we slept outside of the youth hostel that night because there was a...curfew, I don't know, how do you say it?').

Therefore, an Intermediate Mid speaker's Fluency is characterized by extreme to frequent hesitation, extreme brevity, and long pauses. On the other hand, an Advanced speaker's speech sample generally flows with occasional hesitation and a moderate quantity of speech.

---

[9] I am aware that native speakers also hesitate in oral production. For a quantitative study on the amount of pausing that second language acquisition learners produce, see Towell, Hawkins, and Bazergui (1996).

[10] I recommend that future research contain a measure to insure the time length of dysfluent hesitation (Freed, 1995b; Freed, Segalowitz & Dewey, 2004; Segalowitz & Freed, 2004).

Diary entries

I operationalized and measured the learners' social attitudes based on culture-specific comments from their diaries and informal interviews that included positive or negative aspects of: (a) comparisons stating that one culture or system was better or worse than the other; (b) descriptions of Argentines' personalities, actions, or way of life; (c) feelings about a particular situation or event; and (d) comments of new perspectives of the host country, people, or experience. Any comments in these categories are significant since they offer a window into the learners' opinion-formation process.

By making comparisons the learners are compelled to make evaluative comments. For example, the tendency to make more comparisons of inequality by stating that the US culture exceeds that of Argentina in some aspect may be an indicator of a negative social attitude toward the host culture. If that attitude is held constant throughout the diary entries, then a conclusion about the learners' overall social attitude is made. For this study, the learners' culture-specific comments found in their diary entries were tallied and evaluated. If the total number of positive comments was greater than the negative comments, the learner was characterized as possessing a positive social attitude toward the host culture. The opposite was also maintained for learners with a negative social attitude. If the number of positive and negative comments were equal, then the learner was characterized as possessing a neutral social attitude, which did not occur with any of the learner participants.

The learners' motivational orientation was obtained by two means. One means to decide if their motivation was labeled as intrinsic, instrumental, or integrative was based on comments in the initial, pre-program questionnaire that consisted of: (a) personal opinions based on their experience as a whole; and (b) explanations for taking certain actions. The second means of determining motivation to learn the language was by translating the learners' positive or negative attitude to a high or low motivational orientation, respectively. This manner of determining the learners' motivation is more reliable than implementing the usual self-report medium.

Network contact logs

A method of recognizing personal networks is to ask the informants to keep a one-week log of the people with whom they interact (Cubitt, 1973; Gal, 1979; Vann, 1996). The participants were each given seven daily log sheets to fill out and a short page of instructions (see Appendix C). Each day the students recorded: (a) the activities in which they were involved; (b) the name of the person with whom they carried out the activities; and (c) in which language, Spanish or English, the interaction occurred. These log sheets were filled out at three different times during their stay abroad and returned to me during the first, eighth, and fifteenth week.

Chapter 3
QUANTITATIVE RESULTS AND ANALYSES: LINGUISTIC ACCURACY AND ORAL COMMUNICATION SKILLS

In this chapter[11] the data from two sources are analyzed and discussed. The data collected from the SOPI provide the participants' pre- and post-study abroad proficiency levels. I then carried out informal interviews every month during the participants' stay abroad, creating a speech corpus. I analyzed this corpus for development in linguistic accuracy and oral communication skills. On a broader scope, this chapter examines the corresponding development in the learners' oral communication skills in Spanish. The first section reports the development of linguistic accuracy of the five participants as a whole and summarizes the impact that the study abroad experience had on their development of accuracy and oral communication skills. The second section reports the frequencies and discusses the quantitative data for each participant, analyzing the development of linguistic accuracy and correlating it to development seen in oral communication.

Briefly, as detailed in Chapter 2, linguistic analyses of the five speech samples of the participants were performed in order to identify features of fluency and accuracy for the following linguistic elements: (a) appropriate Tense selection (present vs. past); (b) appropriate Aspect selection (imperfect vs. preterite); (c) Subject-Verb agreement; and (d) Gender-Number agreement. I limit the focus to

---

[11] An earlier version of this chapter was previously published as "Development of oral communication skills abroad" in *Frontiers: The Interdisciplinary Journal of Study Abroad*, 9, 149-173.

these syntactic elements since any considerable number of errors in (a) and (b) could hinder comprehensibility (although errors in other elements such as lexicon could also hinder comprehensibility). Errors in (c) and (d) were targeted because accuracy in agreement is an element that shows improvement over time in language learners. These syntactic elements were also focused on since the SOPI guidelines list confusion of aspect and tense selection and agreement errors as markers of distinct oral proficiency levels.

To clarify the analysis of learners' linguistic development throughout the five-month period, slopes of the linguistic accuracies were calculated for all five months abroad. The slopes were calculated not only to show how the learners performed at the beginning and end of their stay but also to illustrate any fluctuation that took place in their linguistic development during their stay abroad, providing a more exact picture as to what occurred in the learners' acquisition process (instead of just having a pre- and post-program analysis). The slopes were calculated through SPSS linear regression tests using the linguistic elements under study as the dependent variable and the month as the independent variable, showing the relationship between these two variables. A positive slope indicates degree of development as opposed to a negative slope that indicates no development. A slope that was closer to zero represents linguistic development with much variation in accuracy across the five months while a slope distant from zero indicates linguistic development with small variation in accuracy across the five months.

I need to note that in describing the learners progress, I list them in raw percentages of accuracy and it would have probably helped the reader to know if moving from an 88% to 99% in Tense selection from Month 2 to Month 3 is significant in any way other than being a trend in the right direction, in other words, statistically significant. I must remind the reader at this point that my initial purpose of this analysis was to show that fluctuation in accuracy was happening month to month, hypothesizing that students would not progress in linear fashion and hoping to see an overall positive progress toward the end of their stay abroad. This explains why, except for the calculation of slopes and SOPI improvement, tests of statistical significance were not carried out for each month in this study.

Table 1 shows the proficiency development over the five months for the five learner participants. In Tables 2 and 3, the reader can see a presentation of the development of learners' linguistic accuracy followed by gains seen in their oral communication skills. Tables 4, 6, 8, 10, and 12 show the percentages of appropriate usage for each of the linguistic elements for the five participants along with their slopes of linguistic accuracy. Tables 5, 7, 9, 11, and 13 show the learners' Fluency and Functions attempted including Simple Narration and Description and Detailed Narration and Description.

In the following sections, the first section displays the scores for the pre- and post-program SOPIs to provide an overall picture of the learners' oral proficiency development. In the subsequent sections, each learner is first profiled based on personal statements in the questionnaires filled out prior to the study. A description is given that particularizes the learner's development in accuracy and relates it to the corresponding development of oral communication in Spanish.

As discussed in Chapter 2, one of the tools used in this study was a SOPI that was given to the learners at the beginning and end of their study abroad experience in order to measure their proficiency before and after the time abroad. Table 1 shows the ratings each participant received at these times:

TABLE 1. Simulated Oral Proficiency Interview Ratings

	Pre-program SOPI	Post-program SOPI
Stan	Intermediate High	Advanced
Tom	Intermediate Mid	Intermediate High
Mark	Intermediate Low	Intermediate High
Sam	Intermediate Mid	Intermediate High
Jennifer	Intermediate Mid	Intermediate Mid

All learners but one showed improvement in their pre- and post-simulated OPI. Stan, Tom, and Sam showed a difference of one level between interviews, Mark showed a difference of two levels, and Jennifer remained at the same proficiency level as when she started.

Discussion of the Linguistic Development of the Group as a Whole

Before discussing the overall linguistic development of the learners, I present the statistical results of the SOPI rate of improvement. The proportion of pre-program SOPI scores was 2 (SD = .71) whereas the proportion of post-program scores was 3 (SD = .71). A paired sample t-test was conducted to assess the statistical significance of the mean difference in proportions of rates across the two tests. The t-test revealed a statistically significant difference between the two sets in proportions of scores, $t(4) = 3.16$, $p < .034$.

The average slope for all the linguistic elements studied here in theoral ability of all learners is a positive slope of 2.28. In other words, the learners' development of linguistic accuracy overall is positive and steady. A positive slope more distant from zero would signify a higher rate of development with little backsliding.

According to research in second language acquisition, acquisition is not a simple process of accumulating linguistic structures. In fact, each structure is subject to a process of gradual development. There have been different terms used to describe this process. For example, according to Ellis (1998, p. 23), acquisition follows a "U-shaped course of development," in which learners may initially display a high level of accuracy only to apparently regress later before finally once again performing in accordance with target-language norms. Some of the learners in this investigation showed much backsliding in their development of linguistic accuracy through the program period. Few learners showed a steady increase with little to no regression; a slope more distant from zero represents less regression. It must be noted that, although backsliding is a normal aspect of second language acquisition, when learners are at Brown's (1995) "third stage" of interlanguage development, they are able to manifest more consistency in producing the second language. For this reason, it was important to calculate the rate of the backsliding (slope) as one more factor that could be used to determine if development occurred in the learners' linguistic acquisition.

In order to show the importance of the rate of backsliding in the learners' development instead of only the rate of linguistic improvement between Months 1 and 5, I now discuss the rate of improved accuracy for the five learners in the four linguistic accuracy categories in terms of backsliding in another section. Table 2 shows the average improvement (ai), which was calculated by subtracting the percentage of linguistic accuracy of Month 1 from that of Month 5.

The average improvements in descending order in linguistic accuracy made by all five learners are: Tense selection (ai=6.28), Aspect selection (ai=2.8), Gender-Number agreement (ai=2.04), and Subject-Verb agreement (ai=2). The two linguistic elements that showed significance in development were Subject-Verb agreement and Tense selection.

The proportion of errors for Subject-Verb agreement for all learners at Month 1 was .05 (SD = .02) whereas the proportion of errors at Month 5 was .02 (SD = .01). A paired samples t-test was conducted to assess the statistical significance of the mean difference in proportions of errors across the two months. The t-test revealed a statistically significant difference between the two months' proportions of errors, $t(4) = .89$, $p < .009$. The proportion of errors for Tense selection at Month 1 was .09 (SD = .03) whereas the proportion of errors at Month 5 was .03 (SD = .02). The t-test revealed a statistically significant difference between the two sets in proportions of errors, $t(4) = 9.79$, $p < .001$. These averages, however, do not take into account the fluctuations in percentage of linguistic accuracy that occurred during the intermittent months. By evaluating only pre- and post-program linguistic development, which is compared by looking at the accuracy score for Months 1 and 5,[12] the question remains whether the learners' development was constant or if any backsliding took place.

---

[12]This is seen in the limited number in second language acquisition study abroad research (DeKeyser, 1991; Huebner, 1995; Lapkin, Hart, & Swain, 1995; Moehle, 1984; Raupach, 1983, 1984; Regan, 1995).

TABLE 2. Average Linguistic Improvement (ai) in Percentages

		Month 1	Month 2	Month 3	Month 4	Month 5	ai
Stan	Tense	93.8	96.1	98.6	96.4	98.6	+4.8
	Aspect	93.3	90.6	89.9	88.2	88.0	-5.3
	S/V	94.2	97.0	97.9	97.1	96.6	+2.4
	G/N	85.2	91.4	88.7	93.4	93.7	+10.9
Tom	Tense	89.6	92.3	90.5	93.8	96.8	+7.2
	Aspect	95.2	92.1	91.3	97.3	96.9	+1.7
	S/V	93.6	93.0	96.5	98.0	97.2	+3.6
	G/N	82.0	82.6	85.8	90.3	93.7	+11.7
Mark	Tense	93.5	88.3	97.4	95.1	98.4	+4.9
	Aspect	67.6	75.0	75.0	65.4	75.0	+7.4
	S/V	97.0	97.6	93.5	100	98.0	+1.0
	G/N	93.3	78.4	91.2	93.8	73.7	-19.6
Sam	Tense	90.1	98.3	97.3	97.6	98.1	+8.0
	Aspect	100	97.5	89.5	96.8	100	0.0
	S/V	97.6	97.1	96.2	97.1	99.0	+1.4
	G/N	84.2	91.3	88.9	88.5	97.9	+13.7
Jenn	Tense	87.8	90.7	88.0	94.2	94.3	+6.5
	Aspect	66.7	96.3	100	95.5	73.3	+6.6
	S/V	94.2	91.5	97.6	94.0	97.2	+3.0
	G/N	80.0	80.3	82.3	83.0	82.4	+2.4

ai = overall average improvement (Month1 subtracted from Month 5), S/V=Subject/Verb agreement, G/N=Gender/Number agreement.

TABLE 3. Average Slopes (ß) of Development for All Learners

	Tense Selection	Aspect Selection	Subject-Verb Agreement	Gender-Number Agreement
Stan	.99	-1.3	.49	1.9
Tom	10.52	.86	1.22	3.11
Mark	10.46	.52	.44	-2.38
Sam	11.06	-.07	.28	2.46
Jennifer	11.06	1.24	.85	.75
Average	8.82	.25	.66	1.17

The slopes in linguistic accuracy in descending order made by participants are Tense selection (ß = 8.82), Gender-Number agreement (ß =1.17), Subject-Verb agreement (ß=.66), and Aspect selection (ß=.25). These slopes signify that the learners showed the most development with less backsliding in Tense selection and the least development with backsliding in Aspect selection. In other words, there was an overall development of linguistic accuracy in the learners' speech during the stay abroad and the slopes for Months 1 through 5 show that the learners had a more linear development, or limited backsliding, for Tense selection.

Not surprisingly, the development of Aspect selection was the most troublesome for the learners. Breiner-Sanders et al. (2000, p. 16) note this difficulty among Advanced Low speakers (one proficiency level higher than four of the five learners in this study), stating that they "demonstrate the ability to narrate and describe in all major time frames (past, present, and future) in paragraph length discourse, but control of aspect may be lacking at times." Terrell and Salgués de Cargill (1979, p. 159) also documented this difficulty with Aspect selection in the following excerpt:

El sistema verbal del español no ocasiona en su mayor parte grandes problemas al anglohablante por lo que respecto a su interpretación semántica. Cuando se llega a la organización semántica de los tiempos del pasado, cambia sin embargo la situación. El uso del *pretérito* y del *imperfecto* supone para el estudiante un grave problema.

On the whole, Spanish's verbal system does not cause problems for the English speaker regarding its semantic interpretation. The situation changes, nevertheless, when it comes to the semantic organization of the past tenses. The use of preterite *and* imperfect *presents a serious problem for the student.*

This difficulty with accurate aspect selection has led to research in this area by Andersen (1990, p. 137) who proposed the Distributional Bias Principle to suggest a source of learners' inappropriate distribution of aspect use. He suggests that native speakers in normal interactions with other native speakers tend to use each verb morpheme with a specific class of verbs.[13] When learners are then exposed to this language of native speakers, they initially interpret this skewed distribution of forms as an absolute characteristic of the forms themselves. In other words, it suggests that the native speaker input, when biased in one direction, can lead the learner to misperceive the meaning and distribution of a particular form that was discovered in the input. This effect, in turn, can lead to acquisition and overgeneralization of an inappropriate morphological form. So, the fact that the learners in this study had the most difficulty with accurate selection of aspect is not surprising. Of importance, however, is that development *was* seen in Aspect selection.

As previously noted, the accuracy in Tense selection included the ability of the learner to differentiate between utterances that needed to be expressed in the present tense versus the past tense. Development of Tense selection had the highest slope, ß=8.82.

---

[13]"Class" here refers to the aspectual class of verbs, including States, Activities, Accomplishments, and Achievements (Doughty, 1979; Smith, 1991; Vendler, 1967).

Quantitative Results for Each Learner

Stan's progress in linguistic accuracy and oral communication

Stan started the study abroad program with a SOPI rating of Intermediate High and ended five months later with a rating of Advanced. The boundary between Intermediate High and Advanced is considered a major boundary because of its difficulty to cross and a SOPI rater differentiates the two by observing different characteristics of the speaker's language. The SOPI raters note if there are many or only some patterned errors in the grammar, if there is any confusion with the use of the preterite and imperfect verb forms, and if there is a high occurrence of agreement errors. Levels of proficiency are also distinguished according to the use of narration.

The data in Table 4 show that Stan's linguistic accuracy in all categories was at 88% and above. They also indicate that Stan had a positive degree of development in Tense selection, Subject-Verb agreement, and Gender-Number agreement. There was a slight backslide at Month 4 for Tense selection when his score dropped from 98.6% to 96.4% accuracy (-2.2%). He recuperated that accuracy in the following month and had an overall slope for Tense selection of .99.

This phenomenon is referred to as "U-shaped behavior" also by Kellerman (1985), in which he states that the participants' accuracy frequency was initially high, then fell, and finally rose again. Brown (1995) describes the process of gradual development in a similar way but gives it the name of "backsliding." This term denotes that it seems as if the learners have grasped a rule or principle, but they regress to some previous stage of interlanguage development in which random errors occur. "Backsliding is a very typical type of acquisition pattern for both first and second language acquisition and usually occurs at the second, or emergent, stage of interlanguage development" (p. 211).

There was an average positive slope of .52 for accuracy in all categories for the five interviews, revealing that Stan did show development with little backsliding. This small slope is due to the fact that he was fairly accurate at the beginning of the program (his average score for linguistic accuracy in all categories shown in Table 4 was 91.6%). Since Stan had a high level of accuracy at the start of the program, any improvement he made toward 100% accuracy would be small relative to the other learners who began at a lower level. This finding is supported by Milleret's (1991, p. 41) conclusion that learners who know less at the beginning of the program can show gains more easily during summer foreign study than can learners who know more. And also by Towell, Hawkins, and Bazergui (1996) whose evidence suggests that other aspects of the advanced learner's oral production ability "'plateau' with respect to speaking rate and articulation rate" (p. 113).

TABLE 4. Stan's Linguistic Accuracy in Percentages

	Month 1	Month 2	Month 3	Month 4	Month 5	Slope
Tense	93.8	96.1	98.6	96.4	98.6	.99
Aspect	93.3	90.6	89.9	88.2	88.0	-1.3
S/V	94.2	97.0	97.9	97.1	96.6	.49
G/N	85.2	91.4	88.7	93.4	93.7	1.9
Average	91.6	93.8	93.8	93.8	94.2	.52

S/V=Subject/Verb agreement, G/N=Gender/Number agreement.

The data indicate that Stan had a negative slope of -1.3 for accuracy in aspect usage. The slope calculation closer to zero indicates that much more fluctuation in accuracy occurred between Months 1 and 5 for Aspect selection, at times showing improvement and at other times backsliding. A slope more distant from zero does not necessarily correlate with more development in accuracy. It is important to note that the number of occurrences in which Stan used the preterite and the imperfect decreased from 60 occurrences in Month 1 to 25 in Month 5.

The number of errors remained relatively the same at between 4 and 7 errors. Since the number of oral speech samples decreased in which aspect differentiation occurred, it appears that Stan's accuracy in aspect usage decreased but, in reality, the accuracy remained the same.

During the first two interviews Stan used the following functions: 3 Simple Narrations, 1 Detailed Narration, and 4 Simple Descriptions. During the last three interviews a difference is seen, because he produced only one instance of Simple Narration but told 9 Detailed Narrations instead of Simple Narrations or Simple Descriptions. He progressed from describing and narrating in a simple style to a detailed style, showing development in his oral communication skills. For example, during Stan's first-month interview (when he had scored an Intermediate High on the SOPI test), the interviewer asked him if he had had any unforgettable experiences while traveling through Brazil. This story can be seen in (3.1).

(3.1) ¿Una experiencia? [...] recuerdo saliendo um era el según, segundo día en Brazil [...]. Fuimos a una fiesta...y um todo el mundo estaba, "oh, un americano, un americano qué cosa!" Estaba, sí, y era muy difícil para um para hablar muchas cosas porque no sabía cómo es la lengua y muchas cosas así. Pero **era muy difícil** [...]. Pero en esta fiesta, la segun, segunda noche en Brazil, había mucha gente enfrente de mí, um esperando [ ] qué, qué tengo que decir. [...] Era, era bueno, era, **era una buena onda** cuando llegué.

*An experience? [...] I remember going out um the secon, second day in Brazil [...]. We went to a party...and um everyone was, "oh, an American, an American, what a thing!" I was, yes, and it was very difficult to um to speak a lot of things because I didn't know the language and many things like that. But **it was very difficult** [...]. But at this party, the secon, second night in Brazil, there were a lot of people in front of me, um waiting [ ] what, what do I have to say. [...] It was, it was good, it was, **it was cool** when I arrived.*

Whereas other learners in the program would reduce the difficulty level of this task by using a list-making strategy, Stan chose to tell a story of his unforgettable experience about the day he first arrived at a friend's house. Stan set up the story with background information and stated that it was his second day in Brazil. In addition to the background information, he gave evaluative statements such as era muy difícil and era buena onda. Both the background information and evaluative statements raised the difficulty of this narrative from simply listing occurrences that happened on his first night in Brazil to telling a story.

Another characteristic that differentiates an Intermediate High from an Advanced speaker, besides using Detailed Narrative structures instead of Simple ones, is the quantity and general flow of the speech. Stan's quantity of speech remained constant through the five months at an average of 22 words per response, with a slight increase at Month 5, as shown in Table 5.

TABLE 5. Stan's Oral Communication Skills

Month	# words per response	# pauses	# times struggled	SN	SD	DN	DD	SO
1	22.6	45	0	1	1	1		
2	21.3	13	0	2	3			2
3	20.7	12	0	1			4	
4	19.5	9	0	1			2	1
5	24.0	4	0				3	1

SN=Simple Narration, SD=Simple Description, DN=Detailed Narration, DD=Detailed Description, O= Opinion with supporting argument.

As previously mentioned, the number of hesitations was tallied to measure the general flow in Stan's speech. In Month 1, Stan had 45 hesitations but, by Month 5, Stan's speech generally flowed with only 4 hesitations.

Tom's progress in linguistic accuracy and oral communication

Tom's oral proficiency in Spanish was rated Intermediate Mid at the beginning of the session and Intermediate High five months later. The data in

Table 6 shows that Tom made significant gains in his accuracy in the tense selection with a positive sharp slope of 10.5.

TABLE 6. Tom's Linguistic Accuracy in Percentages

	Month 1	Month 2	Month 3	Month 4	Month 5	Slope
Tense	89.6	92.3	90.5	93.8	96.8	10.5
Aspect	95.2	92.1	91.3	97.3	96.9	.86
S/V	93.6	93.0	96.5	98.0	97.2	1.22
G/N	82.0	82.6	85.8	90.3	93.7	3.11
Average	90.1	90.0	91.0	94.9	96.2	3.9

S/V=Subject/Verb agreement, G/N=Gender/Number agreement.

In his first interview, his accuracy was low because he preferred to switch to the present tense even when talking about past experiences. An example of this pattern can be seen in (3.2) in which the interviewer asks Tom if he went to a nightclub the night before:

(3.2) Sí, nosotros **fuimos**[preterite] después de ir al cine un otro bar cuando...no había, no **había**[preterite] mucha gente yo, yo **llamé**[preterite] otros amigos y...me **dijeron**[preterite] que **hay** [present] mucha gente en su departamento y, y **van** [present] al boliche todos juntos y yo **fui**[preterite] para preguntar a las chicas si ellas **quieren** [present] ir.

*Yes, we **went**[preterite] after going to the movies another bar when...there weren't, **there weren't**[preterite] a lot of people I, I **called**[preterite] other friends, and...**they told**[preterite] me that **there are**[present] a lot of people in their apartment and, and **they're all going**[present] to the dance club and I **went**[preterite] to ask the girls if **they want**[present] to go.*

Tom started the description about what he did the previous night by using the appropriate past tense of the verbs <u>fuimos</u> 'we went', <u>había</u> 'there was', and <u>llamé</u> 'I called'. Halfway through the description Tom switched to the inaccurate present tense using <u>hay</u> 'there are' instead of <u>había</u> 'there were' and <u>van</u> 'they go' instead of <u>iban a ir</u> 'they were going to go'. He continued with the description and correctly used the appropriate past tense with <u>fui</u> 'I went' <u>quieren</u> 'they want' instead of the appropriate tense querían 'they wanted'.

It can be concluded that during his first few months abroad, Tom was familiar with the past tense forms in Spanish but felt more comfortable with the present tense regardless of the form needed. During his stay abroad Tom started using a different strategy to recant his past experiences, seen during his fourth month in excerpt (3.3).

> (3.3) ...el próximo día salimos en la mañana llegamos a otro pueblo pasamos. Fuimos en bus a otro pueblo. Y...estábamos saliendo para del bus para esperar el bus y alguien, "¡Hola, hola!" de un restaurante y entramos, "hola, nosotros ¿les...conocimos?"...Porque nosotros estábamos caminando afuera de las ruinas y un auto paró, nosotros hablamos con...dos mujeres...y ésta era las dos mujeres y el hombre. Y "Ah, sí, sí, sí, ah yo recuerdo." Y nosotros hablamos...y..."Sí, ¿dónde ustedes van?" "Ahora vamos a Buenos Aires, esta noche vamos a salir de, uh, Tucumán or Jujuy." Y "ah, y ¿vas a viajar más?" "Yo no, yo voy a volver el lunes a los Estados Unidos pero Stan sí." "Sí, si pasas por la Pampa, si querés quedar en mi casa podés hacerlo. Acá es mi dirección, llámame...tengo una casa grande."
>
> *...the next day we left in the morning and arrived in another town. We went by bus to the other town. And...we were getting out of the bus to wait for the bus and someone, "Hi, Hi!" from a restaurant and we went in, "hi, do we know you?"...Because we were walking outside of the ruins and a car stopped and we spoke with two women...and these were the two women and the man. And "Ah, yes, yes, yes, ah, I remember." And we talked...and..."Yes, where are you going?" "Now we're going to Buenos Aires, we're going to leave tonight from uh, Tucumán or Jujuy." And "ah, and are you going to travel more?" "I'm not, I'm going to return Monday to the US but Stan is." "If, if you pass through the Pampa, if you want to stay in my house you can do it. Here's my address, call me...I have a big house."*

In this excerpt Tom switched to the present tense while telling a story in the past only to make direct quotes, which was marked as an acceptable use of the present tense. Although switching from past to present tense is also commonly used in the first language, the SOPI rating guidelines note that when there is a reliance on the present tense, regardless of the form needed in the target language, it is a performance feature of the Intermediate-Mid and -High level.

This narrative technique accounts for Tom's improvement in Tense selection from 89.6% in Month 1 to 96.8% in Month 5 as seen in Table 6. The data also show that Tom made a positive degree of development in the other linguistic aspects.

His average slope for Tense selection was 10.5, showing a strong relationship between Tom's time abroad and his accuracy rate in this category. Tom's accuracy for Aspect selection in Month 1 was 95.2% and in Month 5 was 96.9%, showing a slight increase in accuracy. His close to zero slope for all five months of .86 reveals that there was a weak but positive relationship between his time abroad and Aspect selection accuracy. It also reveals, however, that there was much fluctuation in his accuracy rate for Aspect selection between months, from 92.1% in Month 2 to 97.3% in Month 4 and down to 96.9% in Month 5. Tom's overall average slope for linguistic development was 3.9. In other words, there was a positive relationship between the amount of time Tom spent abroad and his development in linguistic accuracy. A higher slope would have indicated more development with less linguistic backsliding.

At the beginning of the program Tom had an average 90.1% accuracy rate in all categories, but his speech samples included English and non-target-language forms and content was often unclear and disjointed. An example of Tom's use of English, non-language forms, and lack of clarity is seen in (3.4), an excerpt from an interview in Month 2:

> (3.4) T: [...] Porque en Florida, donde yo trabajo con mucho de los, no con pero en los departamentos de muchos *haitians* y, yo oí cuentos de mi cuñado y el vecino de mi cuñado de *haitians* que siempre están en los coches y EERrr, ellos pararon muy rápido para [ ] el coche [slaps hands together] después o atrás para uh, hace un uh accidente. Y ellos reciben dinero or un, alguna vez el vecino de mi cuñado, es un uh bombero, y ellos llegaron a un accidente y habían cuatro *haitians* en el coche sin un uh sin un problema con el coche, no, pero el coche atrás

I: había pe, pegado or al coche y por eso ellos no, no cambiaron la posición, "¡Oh, yo, no, no puedo muver, no puedo muver!"
I: ¿Todos cuatro dijeron esto?
T: Todos cuatros y no había nada malo con el coche, el coche perfectamente. Por eso, no fue posible que el coche atrás pegó muy, muy rápido y por eso ellos tienen, los bomberos tienen que usar uh *the Jaws of Life*...Y ellos destruyeron, destruyeron todo el coche para uh muver la gente porque "oh, oh." Y todo esos cosas. Y no sé.

T: *[...] Because in Florida, where I work with many of the, not with but in the apartments of many Haitians and, I heard stories from my brother-in-law and my brother-in-law's neighbor about Haitians that always are in the cars and EERrrr, they stopped very fast for [ ] the car [slaps hands together] after or behind to uh, make an uh accident. And they receive money or an, one time my brother-in-law's neighbor, he's a uh firefighter, and they arrived at an accident and there were four Haitians in the car without an uh without a problem with the car, no, but the car behind had stu, struck or the car and so they didn't, didn't change the position. "Oh, I, can't, I can't move, I can't move."*
I: All four said this?
T: All four, and there wasn't anything wrong with the car, the car perfectly. And so, it wasn't possible that the car behind struck very, very fast and so they have, the firefighters have to use uh the Jaws of Life...And they destroyed, destroyed the entire car to uh move the people because "oh oh." And all those things. I don't know.

Tom's struggle to use appropriate language forms created difficulty in narrating in the past and in describing or clearly explaining his experiences in Spanish. Problems were evident in his accuracy with Gender-Number agreement and he still preferred to quote people in the present tense, avoiding a more advanced strategy of using the past tense throughout his speech samples. In the first two months, there were various instances when Tom struggled to create appropriate forms. An example can be seen in (3.5) from Month 1 when Tom responds to the questions of what he did the previous night.

(3.5) Sí, nosotros fuimos, después de ir al cine, un otro bar cuando no **hay much,** cuando no **había, no había** mucha gente yo, yo llamé **otros amigos** y me, **me dijo, me dijeron** que hay mucha gente en su departamento y, y van al boliche todos juntos y yo, yo fui para preguntar a las chicas si ellas quieren ir.

*Yes, we went, after going to the movies, another bar when **there isn't** a lot, when **there weren't, there weren't** a lot of people I, I called **other friends** and **he, he told me, they told me** that there are a lot of people at their apartment and, and that they are all going to the dance club together and I, I went to ask the girls if they want to go.*

Tom first used the present tense of the verb <u>haber</u> 'there are', <u>hay</u> 'there is', and then switched to the correct past tense of <u>había</u> 'there were'. Next, he incorrectly produced the third person singular <u>dijo</u> 'he said', which does not agree with the third person plural, <u>otros amigos</u> 'other friends', but then quickly corrected himself and produced the appropriate form, <u>dijeron</u> 'they said'.

By Months 3, 4, and 5, his confidence and knowledge of the language increased and his responses became longer, which can be seen in Table 7.

TABLE 7. Tom's Oral Communication Skills

	Fluency			Functions Attempted				
Month	# words per response	# pauses	# times struggled	SN	SD	DN	DD	SO
1	42.5	14	4		5		1	1
2	35.9	39	3	1	1		1	
3	22	11	0	1	3			4
4	39	7	0	1	1	1		5
5	46	12	0		1	4	1	

SN=Simple Narration, SD=Simple Description, DN=Detailed Narration, DD=Detailed Description, SO=Gives Opinion with supporting argument.

At Month 3 he averaged 22 words per response, at Month 4 the average rose to 39 and, by Month 5, he produced 46 words per response on average. From the beginning of his stay abroad, Tom used functions that normally characterize Intermediate High discourse (Simple Narration and Simple Description) to talk about his experiences. The characteristic that changed in his oral communication skills during the five months was the number of times he attempted more difficult functions, which include Supporting an Opinion and using Detailed Narration and Detailed Description.

During the first month, Tom's speech had 5 occurrences of Simple Description, 1 Detailed Description, and 1 Supported Opinion, showing that he used an Advanced function twice. At Month 4, Tom used 1 Simple Narration, 1 Simple Description, 5 Supported Opinions, and 1 Detailed Narration, peaking four times to the Advanced level. By Month 5, Tom used 1 Simple Description, 1 Detailed Description, and 4 Detailed Narrations, using Advanced level functions 5 times.

Mark's progress in linguistic accuracy and oral communication

Mark's oral proficiency in Spanish was rated Intermediate Low at the beginning of the study abroad program and Intermediate High at the end. Over the five-month period, Mark showed a high degree of development in accuracy of Tense selection in his oral speech samples with a slope of 10.46, seen in Table 8. A positive development was made in Aspect selection with a smaller slope of .52 and in Subject-Verb agreement with a slope of .44.

Although Mark's linguistic percentage difference between Months 1 and 5 show more improvement in Aspect selection (7.4%) than in Tense selection (4.9%), the slope was greater (ß=10.46) in Tense selection as opposed to that of Aspect selection (ß=.52). The slope calculation closer to zero indicates that much more fluctuation in accuracy occurred between Months 1 and 5 for Tense selection, at times showing improvement and at other times backsliding. It is important to point out that a slope more distant from zero does not necessarily correlate with more development in accuracy. My results show that first and last month scores alone do not give a true representation of the learners' development in certain linguistic elements. Instead, the slope gives a clearer indication of progress over time.

TABLE 8. Mark's Linguistic Accuracy in Percentages

	Month 1	Month 2	Month 3	Month 4	Month 5	Slope
Tense	93.5	88.3	97.4	95.1	98.4	10.46
Aspect	67.6	75.0	75.0	65.4	75.0	0.52
S/V	97.0	97.6	93.5	100	98.0	0.44
G/N	93.3	78.4	91.2	93.8	88.7	-1.38
Average	87.9	84.8	89.3	88.6	90.0	2.51

S/V=Subject/Verb agreement, G/N=Gender/Number agreement.

Mark also showed development in accuracy of Subject-Verb agreement (ß=.44) with a somewhat high percentage of 97% when he began the program, which explains the small size of the slope. The linguistic aspect in which accuracy decreased over the five-month period was Gender-Number agreement. By Month 4, Mark's accuracy in Gender-Number agreement fluctuated, dropping from 93% to 78%, then increasing to 91% and showing 93% accuracy by Month 5. This extreme fluctuation in Gender-Number accuracy that occurred in Mark's second month resulted in a negative slope of -1.38.

Besides showing development in the linguistic elements of Aspect selection and Subject-Verb agreement, Mark also showed development in his oral communication skills in Spanish. From the data collected in the informal oral interview conducted during the first month of the study abroad program, Mark struggled to create appropriate forms, which caused his flow of speech to be marked with frequent hesitation. As can be seen in Table 9, the length of his responses tended to be brief. During his first interview in Month 1, there were 6 moments in which Mark struggled with the language. The same was true in the interview in the second month, but a decrease was seen in the following months in which 2 difficulties were noted for Month 3, 1 in Month 4, and none in Month 5.

As Mark became more secure in producing verb forms, the quantity and flow of his speech also improved. The quantity of speech for each response on the average was calculated to be 8.3 words during the interview in Month 1.

TABLE 9. Mark's Oral Communication Skills

	Fluency			Functions Attempted				
Month	# words per response	# pauses	# times struggled	SN	SD	DN	DD	SO
1	8.3	117	7	1	2			
2	9.7	127	6		2			2
3	8.9	92	2	1	1			2
4	15.5	106	1	2	1	1		
5	20.0	70	0	1	2			2

SN=Simple Narration, SD=Simple Description, DN=Detailed Narration, DD=Detailed Description, SO= Opinion with supporting argument.

By Month 2 it increased to 9.7 words, by Month 4 it increased to 15.5 words, and by Month 5 his utterances averaged 20 words per response. The number of hesitations followed a corresponding downward pattern, decreasing from an initial 117 pauses during the first interview, to 92 in the third, and to 70 pauses by the last interview. The fact that the utterance length increased and the number of hesitations decreased during the stay abroad suggests two elements of Mark's oral production improved during this period.

Another aspect of Mark's oral communication skills that was benefited by the study abroad was the slight increase of more difficult functions such as Supported Opinions and Detailed Narrations. Throughout the semester Mark's speech samples, revealed in the interviews, consisted of using Simple Narration and Simple Descriptions to relate his experiences in Argentina. It must be noted that he did not tell many narrations or descriptions, giving 2 or 3 in each interview. He did use more difficult functions at Month 3, however, when he supported 2 Opinions. He used again a more difficult function in Month 4 by telling 1 Detailed Narration. For example, at Month 2 Mark used a Simple Narration, a function characteristic of the Intermediate level, to tell me what he had done the day before, as seen in (3.6):

(3.6) M: Uh...uh fuimos a jugar um básquet. Ayer uh, a la club de amigos uh los hombres de mi programa uh...y después...yo fui a la fiesta de Claire, Miguel y Dave uh a su apartamento...y, es todo.
I: Muy bien. ¿Te gustó la fiesta?
M: Sí, cómo no. Hay muchas personas uh estuvieron allá que uh me gustan uh...hay uh sí, hay muchas tra, tragos, sí. Me gusta mucho de uh su apartamento. Sí.

M: Uh...uh we went to play um basketball. Yesterday uh, at the friends' club uh the men from my program uh...and afte...I went to Claire, Miguel, and Dave's party uh at their apartment...and, that's all.
I: Very good. Did you like the party?
M: Yes, of course. There are a lot of people uh they were there that uh I like them uh...there is uh yes, there are many dri, drinks, yes. I really like uh their apartment. Yes.

Mark lists the activities he did the previous day without giving any detail or evaluative comments, saying that he played basketball with some friends and went to a party. His answers were somewhat brief and he had to be pressed for such details as if he liked the party or not. This excerpt from Month 2 in (3.6) is contrasted with excerpt (3.7) from his fourth interview, in which the interviewer asked him a similar question about what he had done the night before.

(3.7) M: Uh, no, no uh. Fuimos, fuimos a mirar el partido entre Boca y River uh...uh a la Plata.[14] Nosotros tratamos uh obtener, comprar los boletos de River pero ellos uh, uh el estadio, no quedan los, los boletos de River. Solamente ellos tuvieron los boletos de Boca por uh setenta uh pesos.
I: Y, ¿adónde fueron a ver el partido?
M: Recoleta uh World Sports Café, ¿conocés? Sí...estuvo impresionante uh los fascinados allá en el bar. Especialmente los, los aficionados de Boca...uh...sí, estuvo divertido [...]. Uh...ellos no uh...estuvieron gritando y cantando, saltando, todo. Sí. Uh. Tuvo una...pelea un poca pelea, no, no pasó mucho.

M: Uh, no, no uh. We went, we went to see the game between Boca and River uh...uh in the Plata stadium. We tried uh to get, to buy tickets

---

[14]River and Boca Juniors are rival teams in the world of soccer in Argentina.

but they uh, uh the stadium, there aren't any left of the, the River tickets. They only had the Boca tickets for uh seventy uh dollars.
[...]
I: And, where did you go to see the game?
M: Recoleta uh World Sports Café, do you know it? Yes, it was impressive uh the fans there in the bar. Especially, the Boca fans...uh...yes, it was fun [...]. Uh...they no uh...they were yelling and singing, jumping, everything. Yes. Uh. There was a...fight a little fight, no, not a lot happened.

In this excerpt, illustrating a Detailed Narrative, Mark told me, the interviewer, that he went to see a soccer game at a local bar between the two most popular clubs in Buenos Aires. He provides me with more than a discrete listing of the occurrences with explicit description of what impressed him about the soccer fans' behavior during the game. Another important aspect of giving a Detailed Narrative is providing background information. But in this case, we both understood that it would be a *faux pas* for him, a fan of the River team, to sit in the opposing Boca fan section even if that was where the available seats were for a sold-out game. Therefore, instead of explaining why he went to a bar to see the game, he described the wild actions of the soccer fans in the bar.

Nonetheless, Mark showed development in his ability to give a Detailed Narrative in the past. Aspects of this ability can be seen in (3.8) from Month 5:

(3.8) M: [...] fuimos a un pueblo cerca de Corrientes, se me fue el nombre, uh...Patriajias, una cosa así. Uh..., sí. **Estuvo bien.**
I: ¿Por cuánto tiempo fuiste?
M: Uh, el, el fin de semana uh...nada más...uh dos noches de uh camping y dos noches...de uh en micro. Uh...sí uh...pescamos y uh...yo, yo, yo no uh tuve mucha suerte pero uh mis amigos uh...uh...pescaron, pescaron...cuatro o cinco. [...] Um los peces uh estuvieron demasiado pequeño, pequeños. Pero...uh, los peces estuvieron así [shows size with hands] [...]. **Tuvimos mucho suerte porque** [...] encontramos uh, uh...unos tipos que uh tienen una lancha [...]."
I: [...] ¿qué tipo de pez era?
M: Uh, dorado. Es famoso acá el dorado. Sí uh...Tuvimos un pez y uh, nosotros hicimos una parilla de, de madera uh y uh cocinamos el pescado en la parilla y **estuvo mucho divertido y uh, rico también.**

M: [...] we went to a town near Corrientes, the name slipped my mind, uh...Patriajias, something like that. Uh...yes. It was good.
I: For how long did you go?
M: Uh, the, the weekend uh...no more...uh two nights of uh camping and two nights...of uh in a bus. Uh...yes uh...we fished and uh...I, I, I didn't uh have a lot of luck but uh my friends uh...uh...went fishing, went fishing...four or five. [...]. Um the fish there were too small, small. But...uh, the fish were like this [shows size with hands].... **We had a lot of luck because** [...] we found uh, uh...some guys that uh have boat [...]."
I: [...] what type of fish was it?
M: Uh, dorado. The dorado is famous here. Yes uh...yes. We had a fish and uh, we made a grill from, of wood uh and uh we cooked the fish in the grill and **it was lots of fun and uh, delicious too**.

Mark gave a definite past time narrative, in which he included background information and evaluative comments so that I understood the point that was being made in telling the story. He was trying to convey to me why he was very lucky during the camping trip that he had recently taken. Mark's evaluative phrases with which he made that point, included: <u>Estuvo bien</u>, <u>Tuvimos mucho suerte porque...</u>, and <u>estuvo mucho divertido y uh, rico también</u>. Mark transmitted the message that this experience was pleasant for him. Telling a story and explaining why it is a story worth telling is a characteristic of the Detailed Narrative (Polanyi, 1982).

Sam's progress in linguistic accuracy and oral communication
Sam's oral proficiency in Spanish was rated Intermediate Mid at the beginning of the session and Intermediate High at the end. Table 10 illustrates that Sam showed an overall development in the use of the four linguistic elements studied here, starting and ending the program with a good understanding of Aspect selection and Subject-Verb agreement and very little fluctuation in accuracy.

TABLE 10. Sam's Linguistic Accuracy in Percentages

	Month 1	Month 2	Month 3	Month 4	Month 5	Slope
Tense	90.1	98.3	97.3	97.6	98.1	11.06
Aspect	100	97.5	89.5	96.8	100	-.07
S/V	97.6	97.1	96.2	97.1	99.0	.28
G/N	84.2	91.3	88.9	88.5	97.9	2.46
Average	93.0	96.1	93.0	95.0	98.8	3.43

S/V=Subject/Verb agreement, G/N=Gender/Number agreement.

The most improvement was seen in Tense selection and Gender-Number agreement. Although Sam's Tense selection was relatively high in Months 2 through 5, Month 1 showed the lowest accuracy rate of 90.1% for 11 inaccuracies among 111 occurrences of Tense selection. The corresponding ß=11.06 and ß=2.46 scores relate the amount of regression in acquisition that existed in Sam's accuracy rate between the interviews. The slope of 11.06 in Tense selection shows that Sam developed in this category with little backsliding. On the other hand, although Sam did have an overall development in Gender-Number agreement, the backsliding in Months 3 and 4 accounts for the low slope of 2.46. A sample of the grammatical inaccuracies can be seen in (3.9), in which Sam describes the carnival in São Paulo, Brazil.

(3.9) [...] estuve en uh São Paolo los primeros dos días de Carnaval y no podía encontrarlo en São Paolo por eso fui a Río para, para hacerlo. Y...uh, compré una uh bolete para el, uh ¿desfile? Como sambódromo. El último uh noche cual es, supuestamente uh **ser** uh el mejor noche para ir a ver porque **son**[present], o **sean**[subjunctive] las mejores escuelas de samba. Y, en las sambódromos, sambódromo, uh personas bailan todo la noche, es...empieza a las ocho de la noche y termina a las ocho de la mañana. Doce horas **de bailando, tomando, gritando** [...].

*[...] I was in uh São Paolo the first two days of Mardi Gras and I couldn't find it in São Paolo so I went to Rio to, to do it. And...uh, I bought a uh ticket for the, uh parade? Like sambódromo. The last uh night which is, supposedly uh to be the best night to go see because **they***

> *are, or they are the best samba schools. And, in the sambódromos, sambódromo, uh people dance all night, it's...it starts at eight at night and ends at eight in the morning. **Twelve hours of dancing, drinking, yelling [...]**.*

The first Tense selection inaccuracy occurs when Sam uses the infinitive <u>ser</u>, 'to be', instead of the conjugated first-person form, <u>es</u> 'it is'. In the same sentence, Sam switches from the correct present tense of the verb 'to be' <u>son</u>, to the incorrect present subjunctive, <u>sean</u>. These two errors are not patterned and seem to have occurred in a paragraph in which Sam was trying to explain a very exciting event and was not focusing on form at that exact moment. Instead, his priority seemed to get the description of the experience across to the interviewer.

The last errors in this paragraph are transfer errors, reflecting the learner's attempts to make use of his first language knowledge. The gerund of the verb, in this case "dancing," is often used in English after the preposition "of," especially when the sentence is translated, "Twelve hours of dancing, drinking, and yelling." In Spanish, however, the infinitive is always used after prepositions, so the correct forms of the verbs should be <u>bailar, tomar</u>, and <u>gritar</u>. The inaccuracies tallied for Month 1 include errors that are typical of learners with English as their first language.

Sam's score for Gender-Number agreement throughout the semester is similar to the other learners' scores in this study. For most of the learners during the first month, accuracy in Gender-Number agreement was around 80%, whereas the other categories, accuracy was around 90%. Sam showed some backsliding in Months 3 (88.9%) and 4 (88.5%), but by Month 5 (97.9%) his accuracy rate was above that of Month 1 (84%). This pattern corresponds to what various researchers claim as an acquisition order in which grammatical agreement is generally acquired later than other grammatical elements.

Throughout the five-month period, Sam demonstrated development in linguistic accuracy and a slight corresponding development in oral communication skills. The linguistic category that noticeably changed was Sam's fluency. Of the three elements examined in this study that define fluency (quantity of speech, flow of speech, and number of times the participant struggled with appropriate language), Sam showed much improvement in his flow of speech, averaging 32 pauses in Month 1, 16 in Month 3, and 8 in Month 5, as can be seen in Table 11. Throughout the program period, his speech had rare pauses, a characteristic that was matched by only one other student in the program.

TABLE 11. Sam's Oral Communication Skills

	Fluency			Functions Attempted				
Month	# words per response	# pauses	# times struggled	SN	SD	DN	DD	SO
1	16.5	32	1	2	2			
2	18.3	30	0	1			1	4
3	10.9	16	0	1		1		
4	14.0	6	0	1	1			1
5	13.4	8	0		2			2

SN=Simple Narration, SD=Simple Description, DN=Detailed Narration, DD=Detailed Description, SO= Opinion with supporting argument.

Although Sam demonstrated improvement in flow of speech, his utterances were very often quite brief, with a mean average of 13.4 words per response during the last interview. This mean was the lowest utterance length of all students for the last interview. He often answered the interviewer's questions with minimal detail and tended to utter single sentences. He rarely produced utterances that provided important information to allow the listener to know why the story was important, an element that would be necessary to categorize his speech sample as a Detailed Narration or Detailed Description.

Jennifer's progress in linguistic accuracy and oral communication

Jennifer's oral proficiency in Spanish was rated Intermediate Mid at the beginning of the session and she left five months later with the same rating of Intermediate Mid.

The data in Table 12 show that, although Jennifer remained at the same proficiency level, she had an average slope of 1.12, indicating a positive degree of development in linguistic accuracy without much backsliding. Since Jennifer started the program with a lower accuracy rating in the four categories, however, a steeper slope showing improvement was needed in order to be rated at the next level of Intermediate High.

TABLE 12. Jennifer's Linguistic Accuracy in Percentages

	Month 1	Month 2	Month 3	Month 4	Month 5	Slope
Tense	87.8	90.7	88.0	94.2	94.3	1.65
Aspect	66.7	96.3	100	95.5	93.3	1.24
S/V	94.2	91.5	97.6	94.0	97.2	.85
G/N	80.0	80.3	82.3	83.0	82.4	.75
Average	82.2	89.7	92.0	91.7	91.8	1.12

S/V=Subject/Verb agreement, G/N=Gender/Number agreement.

Jennifer was able to talk about herself in simple conversations such as her personal history, but she did not use more difficult functions of Detailed Description or Detailed Narration to convey her experiences. Although there were quite a few instances of supporting an opinion and several instances of using the past tense to tell stories in the past, a function categorized as more difficult, she lacked paragraph-length utterances and it was laborious for her to sustain her speech during the interviews.

In other words, she was not able to say much about her experiences. An example can be seen in the following excerpts (3.10) and (3.11) taken from an interview that took place during the last two months of the study abroad program. I asked Jennifer to tell of any interesting trips she took in the last month:[15]

(3.10) I: [. . .] ¿Viajaste durante este último mes?
J: Um...no. Fuimos, yo, yo sólo fui a un viaje a Iguazú...fue muy lindo. [. . .]
I: Y, ¿cómo estuvo?
J: Um...muy, muy lejos [laughs] pasábamos um dieciocho horas en un micro y el día que uh...cuando fuimos al cataratas estaba lloviendo...y, pero **fue increíble**. Muy, muy impresionante las cataratas.

I: [...] Did you travel this past month?
J: Um...no. We went, I, I only went on a trip to Iguazú...it was very nice. [...]
I: And, how was it?
J: Um...very, very far [laughs] we spent eighteen hours in a bus and the day that uh...when we went to the waterfalls it was raining...and, but **it was incredible**. Very, very impressive the waterfalls.

In another instance during the same interview, I asked Jennifer the same question with the purpose of eliciting more details:

(3.11) I: [...]. ¿Viajaste a algún lugar?
J: Sí, a la quinta este fin de semana con mi familia.
I: Y, ¿cómo estuvo?
J: Muy lindo. Tienen una casa y con piscina y hicimos asado afuera, y tomaron sol y...fue muy lindo. **Me gustó**.

I: [...] Did you travel somewhere?
J: Yes, to the country house this weekend with my family.
I: And, how was it?
J: Very nice. They have a house and with a pool and we had a barbecue outside, and they sunbathed and...it was very nice. **I liked it**.

Jennifer spent a week at the impressive Iguazú Falls and had to be nudged for any details. The same was true when the interviewer asked Jennifer to describe one of

---

[15] The interviewer allowed much time for Jennifer to expand on her answers. When it was noted that Jennifer was not going to give more detail, the interviewer tried to help her by asking questions focusing on a possible story line.

the occasions in which she enjoyed herself. Although she did use evaluative statements such as fue increíble and me gustó her quantity of speech per response was low. Jennifer averaged 14 words per response throughout the five-month period, one of the lowest for the group of participants. The general flow of her speech was hindered by an average of 39 hesitations per interview, as shown in Table 13.

TABLE 13. Jennifer's Oral Communication Skills

Month	# words per response	# pauses	# times struggled	SN	SD	DN	DD	SO
1	12	61	1	2	2			3
2	14	54	2	1	1			2
3	12	31	0		2			3
4	14.9	14	0		1			5
5	14.7	33	0		1			2

SN=Simple Narration, SD=Simple Description, DN=Detailed Narration, DD=Detailed Description, SO= Opinion with supporting argument.

This pattern reflected the description of the ACTFL Guidelines for an Intermediate Mid speaker that "the smooth incorporation of even basic conversational strategies is often hindered as the speaker struggles to create appropriate language forms" (Byrnes & Canale, 1987, p. 16). The two excerpts in (3.10) and (3.11) are representative of Jennifer's oral communication, characteristically marked by brevity of words.

Development in learners' oral communication skills is measured here by the ability to attempt more difficult functions such as Support an Opinion, which consistently did, and uses of Detailed Narration and Detailed Description. Throughout the five months, Jennifer preferred to use Simple Narration and functions normally used by Intermediate speakers. But the occurrence of the Simple Narrations and Simple Descriptions were limited because there were 2 occurrences of each in Month 1, one of each in Month 2, 4 Simple Descriptions in Months 3, 4, and 5, and 1 Simple Narration in Month 2.

Discussion

Here I present a holistic analysis of the production by the entire group of participants. In the first section the learners' linguistic development is discussed according to the amount of development seen in conjunction with the amount of linguistic fluctuation, or backsliding, that occurred during the stay abroad. The succeeding section then recaps the linguistic accuracy development findings and connects them with the learners' development in oral communication skills.

Oral communication skills and linguistic development

In this section, a broad picture is presented of what occurred in the development of oral communication skills for the learners and is linked to linguistic accuracy findings. As mentioned in Chapter 2, the learners' communication strategies were noted throughout the five months. The following elements that can indicate positive development in the learners' oral communication skills in Spanish were noted: an increase in meshing descriptive background with the sequential recounting of events and providing sensorial richness and explicitness when telling a description; quantity and flow of utterances in terms of hesitations and pauses; and the ability to give supported opinions.

Throughout his five interviews, Stan progressed from a preference for simple functions to narrate and describe experiences to the use of more elaboration and explicitness. These functions that Stan preferred to implement toward the end of his stay abroad are characteristics of advanced oral ability. This preference implies that Stan learned to utilize storytelling strategies, as opposed to list-making strategies, to narrate his experiences.

Stan showed a positive development in his accuracy of the studied linguistic elements. His oral communication skills also developed, as evidenced by the fact that he improved from using a simple oral communication style to describe and narrate events to a more detailed one. In addition, the fluency aspect of Stan's oral communication skills showed positive development: his speech during the interviews flowed with rare pauses (45 at the beginning of the program to 4 at the end) and included a fair quantity of speech (averaging 21.6 words per sentence) for the questions asked.

Tom struggled to keep his narratives in the past tense, preferring to avoid the problematic choice between the preterite versus the imperfect aspect by using the present tense. This preference is not to be confused with the aforementioned alternation between the past tense and the historical present. The tense errors found in Tom's narratives were not of this kind. The transcriptions of the interviews show that when Tom alternated between the past tense and the historical present there was a change in intonation or a brief pause before the direct quote.

Overall, the data show that Tom improved in his linguistic accuracy during the semester abroad. He also showed a corresponding development in his oral communication skills because he produced a good quantity of speech for the tasks, his narratives were coherent and clear, and he preferred to forego simpler narrative strategies of listing occurrences for more advanced ones, such as telling a story, starting at his fourth month abroad. We can conclude that the study abroad experience started to benefit Tom's oral communication skills during his third month abroad.

Mark's oral communication skills developed throughout the study abroad program, as evidenced by various factors. First, Mark's flow of speech toward the end of the program was marked with only occasional hesitations as compared to the beginning in which he hesitated intermittently throughout his interviews. A second factor that illustrates development in Mark's communication skills was the increase in the quantity of speech in his responses at the end of the program. A third factor was that he *attempted* to use some advanced functions toward the middle of the program and became more confident with verb forms, as was evidenced by his accuracy of the various linguistic elements examined.

Again, we can conclude that Mark's oral skills were somewhat benefited by five months studying abroad, his fluency increased and he started to pull away from using the simpler narrative strategies to making an effort to put newly acquired communication skills to use. Although these attempts were not numerous, we can assume that Mark was overcoming his insecurities with the language and starting to be a moderate risk-taker in practicing the language. And as noted by Rubin (1975), "good language learners are willing to guess, willing to appear foolish in order to communicate, and willing to use what knowledge they have of the target language in order to create novel utterances." Beebe (1993) termed Rubin's description of a good language learner as having "risk-taking behaviours," exactly what Mark showed when he was abroad.

Sam's performance shows that he focused on the production of accurate grammar, illustrated by his high accuracy rate. He frequently focused little on the content of his speech, as seen in his brief responses that did not elaborate on topics. Due to this tendency, Sam responded to my questions, telling me what happened with minimal information and did not include descriptive background information that explained why it took place. During the second month, however, there was one occasion when he elaborated with explicitness of description and one occasion during the third month when he meshed descriptive background with a sequential recounting of events.

Toward the end of her stay abroad, Jennifer's data show that, although there was positive development in her linguistic accuracy no development was seen in her frequency to produce the advanced functions of a detailed narration or description. Although her fluency did improve, she did not struggle to create appropriate language forms: her number of pauses decreased and the mean number of words uttered remained at almost the same as from the beginning.

Taking a closer look at Jennifer's data, she did not switch from using the simpler form of narrating and describing to the more complex and detailed form of narrating and describing events. Jennifer's speech flow improved and quantity of utterances remained at almost the same level throughout the five months, that is, her fluency was characterized with brief utterances.

So, did Jennifer show development in overall oral communication skills during the semester abroad? Yes, she did show a consistent use of supporting opinions but more detailed narration or description requires more speech than a simple one in order to give more elaborate background information or add evaluative comments. In Jennifer's case, her brief responses did not usually allow for elaboration on any topics. During the ethnographic interviews, she did not seem to treat the interviews as a chance to share her experiences, something that she did do at length in her English written journals. Jennifer may have felt that she lacked vocabulary to express exactly what was on her mind and, instead of trying to circumlocute in order to express these thoughts, she stopped her speech production to avoid any difficulty.

Jennifer was also very sensitive to rejection from the host culture, and when she did feel rejected, as evidenced by her journal entries, that is when her active participation with native speakers started to dwindle (will be addressed in Chapter 4). Naiman, Fröhlich, Stern, & Todesco (1978) support this reaction, they hypothesize that language learners that are sensitive to rejection may avoid active participation in language class, which translates into less successful language acquisition. And although Jennifer was not in a language class, we can easily extend Naiman et al.'s hypothesis to the study abroad environment to explain her behavior.

Summary

This chapter has presented the quantitative findings of this research in terms of the learners' development in linguistic accuracy and oral communication skills. I have seen that different linguistic elements analyzed in this study take varying amounts of time to develop. Accurate tense selection was the linguistic element in which the learners improved the most overall. The time abroad also positively affected accuracy development in gender-number agreement and subject-verb agreement, but the overall development was not as notable as that of tense selection, suggesting that agreement is a linguistic element that takes a little longer to develop. The linguistic element that showed the least positive development abroad was that of aspect selection.

It was also shown that the learners' interlanguage was frequently restructured, seen in the amount of fluctuation in their linguistic accuracy during the five-month stay abroad. Backsliding in the four linguistic elements occurred but did not hinder the overall development of their linguistic accuracy. The development in accuracy of these elements shows that learning a language abroad takes work and that the linguistic variable change does not improve in a linear fashion. This finding provides negative evidence for five to six-week summer study abroad programs that claim that linguistic acquisition takes place.

Finally, it was shown that the learners' development in oral communication skills varies depending on the learner, some used more advanced speech functions whereas others maintained their use of simpler functions. Quantity and flow of speech were the elements of the learners' overall oral communication skills that showed most development over the five-month study abroad period. This phenomenon does not have only one but various interconnected explanations, some of which will be discussed in the next chapter. The development in the use of more complex speech functions is not regulated and learners will advance with time and practice if they are willing to interact with the host culture.

Chapter 4
QUALITATIVE RESULTS AND ANALYSIS: ATTITUDES AND SOCIAL NETWORKS

It must be noted that distinct aspects of the experience abroad influence other aspects. For example, the learners' social attitudes, motivation, and confidence interact with the building of social networks and vice versa. The learners may initially have had a very positive attitude toward the host culture and been motivated to integrate themselves into the new community but may have perceived rejection when they came into contact with Argentine social circles. This rejection may contribute to stagnation in a stage of cultural awareness in which there is no acceptance of the new host culture. After repeated attempts at trying to enter Argentine circles and failing to do so, a negative attitude toward the host culture natives may be created and reinforced by the student.

Overall, it was seen that the type of motivation the learners had in learning the target language, the attitude that they maintained toward the host culture in their diaries, and the strength of their social networks were all connected. This aspect is important to explain one crucial reason why variation exists among the individual learners' processes in second language acquisition. One could posit that variation could be caused by the fact that some of the learners in the program were lazy or not intelligent. We must keep in mind, however, that the students that participate in study abroad programs go through a selection process based on instructor recommendation letters and grade point average. It would be rare in this study abroad program, therefore, for a university to sponsor a learner that would be considered below average.

What was shown was that some learners' diary excerpts started out on a positive note but, throughout the five months, a change to a negative attitude was seen. On the other hand, other learners' attitudes remained neutral or positive throughout the process with fluctuations of negativity depending on the circumstances. All learners invariably felt frustrated at one point or another during the program but it is interesting to note how these situations were dealt with in different manners depending on the individual learner. There are many learner characteristics, such as language learning strategies, extrovertedness, motivation, and attitude, that affect the acquisition process, many of which cannot be controlled or even measured in such a study. The methodology used here attempts to accomplish such a feat: to measure and observe specific learner characteristics and extrinsic factors that are operating on language acquisition in the study abroad context.

This chapter presents discussion of the five participants' social networks in the host country along with excerpts and analyses of their diary entries. In each section, such extralinguistic features as instances of positive or negative motivation and attitude are examined. As outlined in Chapter 2, the learners' attitudes were operationalized and evaluated based on culture-specific commentary about their experiences and the host culture that appeared in their diary entries and informal interviews. I then translated the attitude to a low or high motivational orientation, which I believe is more reliable than self-reported motivational scores. The individual learner's motivation and attitude are mentioned at the beginning of each section and are followed by excerpts taken from diary entries and informal interviews.

In addition, the specific data from the network contact logs, which include the daily activities of the learners (see in Appendix C), indicate the influence that social networks have on language acquisition. The breadth of the social networks, along with the learners' extralinguistic features that were measured in this study, are then compared with the learners' linguistic development discussed in Chapter 3.

Let me briefly review here how I have extended Milroy's (1987) theory of uniplex and multiplex networks to the study abroad environment. Firstly, "network zones" are important to understanding the role that social networks play in successful interaction. Learners in the host country who do not interact with the host culture but rather form closed or dense, multiplex networks with other English-speaking learners will interact mostly within this English-speaking territory. All their contacts will be with one another, making their role relationships multiplex. This dense, multiplex network structure with other study abroad learners will slow down the development of these learners' interlanguage toward a close approximation with the target language. The optimal situation is to have a dense, multiplex network structure with native Spanish-speakers.

On the other hand, study abroad learners who have open personal networks, moving outside the first language English-speaking territory of their fellow study abroad acquaintances, will attain contacts in the host culture, presumably with native speakers. The open network tie is understandably *uniplex* since they have just arrived to a country where they have to build relationships within a new social network, usually starting with one member at a time. Even when the learner is housed with a family and seems to have easier access to a new social network, it does not preclude the fact that the relationships with the new members still have to be built.

When referring to 1st order and 2nd order zones, the persons who are directly linked to X (learner) are characterized by Milroy (1987, p. 46) as "belonging to his *first order* network zone." Each of these people may be in contact with others whom X does not know, but with whom X could come into contact with via the first order zone. These more distantly connected persons form X's "*second order* zone." The learners in the extended (2nd order) networks with native speakers, as opposed to those in the closed (1st zone) networks of other study abroad English-speaking learners, will acquire a set of linguistic norms that are enforced by exchange with those native-speaker contacts.

The concluding section includes a discussion of the predictability of the breadth of social networks and positive diary entries and their link to development in linguistic accuracy and oral communication skills.

Qualitative Analyses and Discussion for Each Learner

Stan's attitudes and social network

Stan's overall disposition during the study abroad program was positive, as was noted in his weekly diary entries. Stan, whose pre- and post-program SOPI ratings were Intermediate High and Advanced, respectively, had a positive attitude towards his experiences in Buenos Aires and had high motivation to study Spanish and understand the new culture. He was continually eager to experience the "real, big-city" life of Buenos Aires but also to see the very distinct culture of "interior" Argentina. His eagerness to learn more about the culture correlated with his high motivation to learn Spanish. He wanted to go beyond just learning the language to get the full meaning of what it meant to be Argentine. Stan's goal of understanding Argentine identity demonstrates his "investment" (Peirce, 1995) to learn the target language, proving that he had multiple desires during his stay abroad.

In the diary entry excerpt (4.1) from Week 1, it can be seen that Stan is not just comparing the US and Argentine social scenes, a topic that was suggested as a diary entry. Stan goes beyond just a physical description of what he sees in a nightclub in Buenos Aires and categorizes the place as something "Argentine." Stan describes an upper-class bar in Buenos Aires. In doing so, he shows that he can identify an aspect of what it means to be Argentine. He believes he is getting to know what the Buenos Aires upper class is like and is confident to state, within his first month, what porteños 'inhabitants of Buenos Aires' appreciate.

(4.1) We got there after an expensive cab ride to Palermo and it was high class. People were in their thirties plus and it was not my kind of place--fancy glass tables, swimming pool--totally out of a VISA commercial or something: two women sitting on a couch sipping champagne, the bathroom was in totally bronze. This was porteños type of place—we Americans thought it was a bar with no cover, our type of place--for porteños this was a good place to go--of course this was the upper crust of porteños but still [...]. (Month 1)

Although Stan points out that this bar "was not my kind of place," he comments about it without making any derogatory remarks. He states that it is different from his personal tastes and notes, "for porteños this was a good place to go." He accepts the difference without making any judgments of the people. In the same diary entry, Stan proceeds to describe his reaction at the show of wealth in this particular nightclub and is surprised by Argentine wealth. It is evident that he has some preconceived notions of how most Latin Americans live.

(4.2) These people have a lot of money--Latin Americans cannot be this wealthy--it must be a front--it appears like this whole city is wealthy which cannot be--I need to explore and see the real side of this city--New York has the high class societies too--every city does but does not cover up the others. (Month 1)

He states an opinion of disbelief and curiosity. Most newly arrived learners give this opinion in reaction to the common stereotype that all countries of Latin America are "Third World." He accepts the fact that there is a wealthy side to Buenos Aires and, at this point in the semester, extends this characterization to describe the rest of Buenos Aires, by writing that "it appears like this whole city is wealthy which cannot be."

But Stan wants to become acquainted with the other side, the one that is "covered up," where he will probably see a different set of values and lifestyles. This upper class of porteños described in (4.2) was displaying features of a culture he already knew, the culture of big-city Americans. The fact that he compares the bar scene to a VISA credit card commercial shows that he is already familiar with what that high-lifestyle is like but he wants to learn something different. Stan went to study abroad not only to learn a new language, but also to learn about the culture that is associated with it. To accomplish this goal, Stan ventured out from his group of American study abroad friends to make connections with Argentines.

Seven weeks into the semester Stan decided to initiate and maintain correspondence with an Argentine whom he had met previously in the US. Stan took up an invitation to visit this individual in Cordoba, a city in the interior, also with the intention of traveling and visiting other cities. He visited Cordoba and Rosario, two cities to the west of Buenos Aires, and became acquainted with the "interior"[16] of the country. By traveling to these cities Stan became acquainted with the "other side" that he had been hoping to find. Excerpt (4.3) details his experience during and after the trip.

(4.3) This past weekend I went to Cordoba and also stopped in Rosario. I spent two days in a friend of a friend's home, which was really nice. The people seemed very different than porteños [...] I almost think it might be better to get to know the 'real' Argentina outside of Buenos Aires...It was good to spend a weekend with a family, to see how they interact and their lifestyle [...] I think I have a better idea of Argentina, of course more trips are necessary to improve the idea even more. (Month 2)

Stan has come into contact with another aspect of the Argentine culture. He has come to realize that his cultural experiences in Buenos Aires represented only one aspect of Argentina. Pointing out that "the people seemed very different than porteños," he shows that, at this point in the semester, he is aware of a distinction within the Argentine culture that he had not previously known: the unmistakable difference between porteños and "interior" non-porteños.

During his eighth week in the program, he proceeds to describe a frustrating experience of checking out a book for research from the National

---

[16]Porteños are stereotyped by the rest of Argentina as being cold and arrogant whereas the rest of the country is very hospitable and warm.

Library of Buenos Aires.

(4.4) Yesterday I had the most frustrating experience yet in Argentina--I went to the national library. Just getting in was a hassle and then trying to get information was so frustrating. I saw card catalogs for the first time in a couple of years but there were a few computers--nearly not enough [...]. There were computer monitors that display your name when your books (Max. 3) are ready. So we're sitting there waiting for our names to appear [...] but the Argentines are just hanging out--when our books are ready, mine are from the 60s and we learn we can't borrow them--At this point I was fed up but we moved to periodicals [...]. When the stack arrived I was about to laugh. A bundle of old newspapers with a string around it! [...] I was so frustrated [...]. (Month 2)

Stan recognizes the difference between the rapidity of gaining information in a library in the US compared to the slow retrieval process in an Argentine library. At this point in the program Stan seems to preserve the hegemony of the American culture over that of Argentina, the second stage of Bennett's (1986) description of ethnocentrism. This observation is noted when he writes that, "I suppose I am used to getting what I want pretty quickly, with little hassles--American way." This statement clarifies Stan's image of the American culture being more efficient and trouble-free, as opposed to that of Argentina, which, in his opinion, is not so, reinforcing his view of the dominance of the more efficient American culture over the inefficient Argentine culture.

Stan differs from some of his fellow students because he does not stop his thought processes at the hegemonic remarks stated in excerpts (4.3) and (4.4). Stan appears to be in the third and last stage of movement toward ethnorelativism when he minimizes the difference between the Argentine and North American cultures and realizes that he is reacting in a particular manner due to his living expectations, seen in excerpt (4.5). Stan specifies what characteristics he must attain in order to accomplish certain things in Argentina.

(4.5) The library could of been worse--there were computers and it was pretty nice, but I am used to an "information society" with easy access to all sorts of info--here patience and time are needed in order to accomplish many things that are easily accomplished in the US. (Month 2)

Stan was able to separate everyday difficulties from his perception of the Argentine culture. The fact that Stan had become culturally aware and accepted and understood some cultural differences, as evidenced by his diary entry (4.5) during Week 8, shows Stan's movement from ethnocentrism to that of ethnorelativism, according to Bennett's (1986) model of acculturation. In other words, the fact that Stan now had a greater recognition of the Argentine culture and accepted the fact that there were differences between the US and Argentina facilitated his ability to form social networks in Argentina. This movement that Stan made from a state of ethnocentrism, in which he denied the existence of cultural differences, to a state of ethnorelativism, is evidenced in Stan's reactions to different situations that are excerpted from his diary entry. The fact that Stan made an effort to minimize the differences between the two cultures reflects the positive attitude that he maintained throughout the study abroad program.

Figure 4. Stan's Language Choice Over Time in Social Situations

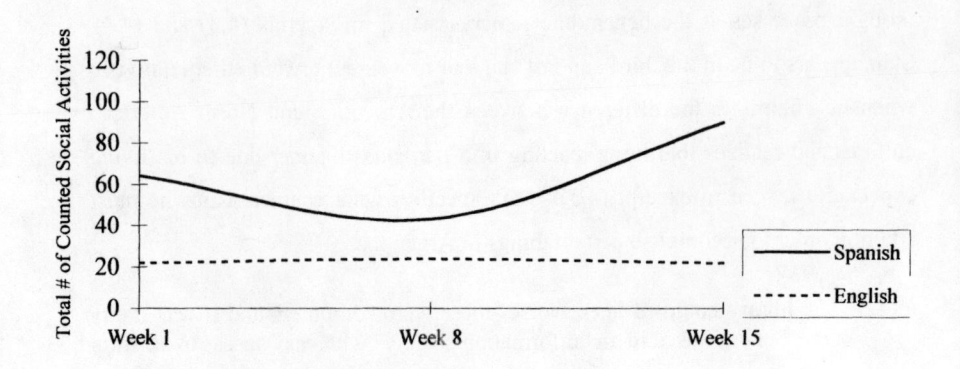

I now discuss Stan's social networks with Argentines. Stan lived in a university apartment with two North Americans and one Mexican and, according to his Social Network Log, spoke more Spanish than English in his social activities with his roommates and other acquaintances. This language choice can be seen in Figure 4. During his first week he tended to socialize with his North American friends but Spanish was the language of choice over English, accounting for the few number of Argentines in his social network, as can be seen in Table 14 and represented in Figure 5.

TABLE 14. Stan's First and Second Order Zone Social Networks

SOPI rating	Month	1st order zone uniplex Argentine members	2nd order zone multiplex Argentine members
IH	1	1	
	2		
	3	3	3
	4		
A	5	3	5

SOPI=Simulated Oral Proficiency Interview, IH=Intermediate High, A=Advanced.

Figure 5. Stan's (X) First and Second Order Zone Social Networks

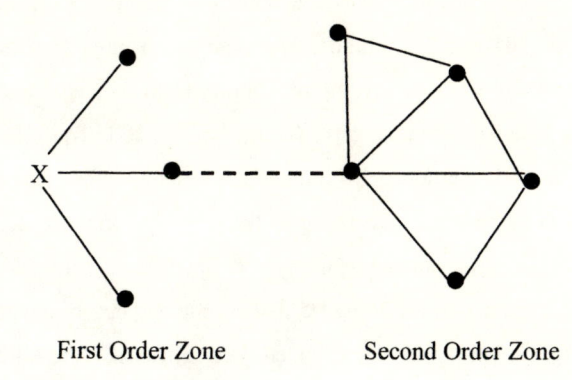

First Order Zone   Second Order Zone

As noted earlier, Stan stayed in contact during his stay in Argentina with a friend of a friend who lived in Cordoba, a city about ten hours from Buenos Aires. By Month 3, as tallied from his self-reported network contact logs, Stan had a social network of six Argentine friends; three were members of his first order zone, uniplex social network (see discussion of these in Chapter 2) and three were members of his second order zone, multiplex social network. He entered into the second order zone through the friend of a friend who then introduced Stan to his two friends, and included him in activities with them.

By Month 5, Stan had already taken two trips to Cordoba and, consequently, his second order zone social network increased to five people due to the new friends he made during those two visits. These new friends also came to visit him in Buenos Aires and were all planning a trip to Chile in the following months. According to his network contact log, when he was socializing with both the North Americans and the Argentines, which was in Spanish most of the time, it was not uncommon for him to argue a point with a friend or to tell a story.

As measured from his diaries and informal interviews, Stan's positive attitude and high motivation were factors in the maintenance and development of his social networks while in Argentina from that of a first order zone to that of the preferred second order zone. By the last month, the latter consisted of friends in Buenos Aires and close friends from Mendoza and Cordoba. Stan's second order zone social network, his positive attitude, and high motivation correlate with changes seen in his linguistic accuracy and oral ability from the beginning of the program. His high linguistic accuracy gave Stan, who wanted to learn the "real" side of Argentina, the self-confidence to initiate and sustain different topics and use a range of speech functions from early on in the program. In these situations, it is assumed that Stan was able to elaborate in Spanish on more advanced conversation topics such as politics in the US and narrate and describe with some detail about his experiences. Stan was frequently in situations where he could learn and put into practice different communication skills. Based on Gass and

Varonis' (1994) work mentioned in Chapter 2, these social situations allowed Stan to participate in interactions in which he was able to detect discrepancies between his language and that of the target language, giving him the opportunity to restructure his second language knowledge. Accordingly, the more frequently that Stan participated in these social interactions, the more restructuring occurred, leading to development in his linguistic accuracy over time.

In the previous chapter, it was shown that Stan's linguistic accuracy in oral narratives was already high when he started the program at 91.6% and it improved slightly to 94.2% by the end of the program. It was also shown that Stan's slope in linguistic accuracy was positive, $\beta = .52$. What did noticeably improve, and what can be corroborated by the fact that Stan could handle topics of current and public interest with the native Spanish-speaking members of his social network, was the implementation of speech functions characteristic of the ACTFL Advanced level, such as detailed narrations and descriptions, and development in oral fluency.

Stan differed from some of his fellow students because he understood the difficulty of incorporating oneself in a new culture, as seen in excerpt (4.6) taken from an informal interview at the end of the fourth month abroad.

(4.6) [...] Yo creo que esta experiencia no está bastante. No fue bastante tiempo [por]que el semestre es muy corto [...]. No es una experiencia de académica y [...] bueno, puede ser cultural [...]. Yo entiendo que es difícil, las cosas. Y especialmente para [...] llegar en la cultura. En la universidad es imposible, entonces OPII hizo la mejor cosa que ellos podían hacer. (Month 4)

[...] I think that this experience was not enough. It was not enough time because the semester is very short. [...] It is not an academic experience and [...] well, it could be a cultural one. [...] I understand that it is difficult, things. And especially to [...] arrive into the culture. In the university it is impossible, then OPII did the best thing that they could do.

Stan was able to separate any frustrations he had with the academic system from the Argentine culture. He was open to understanding and accepting the host culture. His curiosity to learn more about Argentina allowed him to be flexible, accepting any situation that would lead him to acquire knowledge about the country, such as friends' invitations to their country homes.

Stan's ability to reach the later stages of ethnorelativism and to minimize cultural differences reflected the positive attitude that he maintained throughout the study abroad program. I posit that this attitude was the basis for why Stan showed development in linguistic accuracy and oral communication skills. I also posit that this attitude and his social network correlate with his high degree of development in functions of oral ability over time.

Tom's attitudes and social network

During his first four weeks in Argentina, Tom, whose pre- and post-program SOPI scores were Intermediate Mid and Intermediate High, respectively, lived with an Argentine host family in an affluent part of Buenos Aires. They included him in family meals and social outings. When the school semester started, Tom moved into student housing and lived with a French student since the family he lived with had made plans, prior to his arrival, for another student to live with them. The two roommates spoke Spanish when addressing each other. In his first-month diary entries, Tom made many comparisons between Argentina and the US, a topic that had been suggested at the beginning of the study. He tended to make neutral comparisons that dealt with elements that were usually experienced abroad, such as the lack of importance of punctuality in Latin American countries.

> (4.7) First major difference I noticed between Argentina and the US is the amount of organization each country has. I have found that people seem to be unorganized here and time is not all that important [...]. Although there seems to be room for improvement in these areas [of apparent disorganization], it has been an enjoyable experience [...].

> All in all it has been an eye-opening experience that I'm enjoying and believe will teach me a lot about people and life [...]. Have to say that I am pretty impressed with transportation here. (Month 1)

Tom also made suggestions during his first month to help Argentina's fragile economic status, as in excerpt (4.8).

> (4.8) I think our system of those who can pay for college paying and those who can't applying for financial aid might be a little better because then not everyone goes for free. This might save some money for government. (Month 1)

Another diary excerpt that reveals Tom's positive attitudes toward the new host culture and experience abroad, notable for its lack of negative remarks, is one in which he experienced an occurrence in Argentine classrooms that he had been warned about; that professors sometimes do not show up to teach. Instead of making a criticism, he made the following comment:

> (4.9) This is something my friend, Heidi, had warned me about. But truthfully, I am here to improve my Spanish, live in a different culture, learn about another country, travel, and have a good time. I think that even if I don't learn much in class I will learn a lot just by living here. Just wanted to add that. (Month 1)

In excerpts (4.6) to (4.9), Tom recognized the cultural differences between Argentina and the US and at times preserved the hegemony of the US culture over that of Argentina. An example of this recognition is seen in his advice on how Argentina could have a more stable economic system, like that of the US. But Tom also acknowledged the possibility of differences among cultures and adapted to the environment by separating some of the cultural differences for the sake of improving his Spanish and learning about another culture, as he states in excerpt (4.10) taken from his first month diary entries:

(4.10) All in all, it has been an eye-opening experience that I'm enjoying and believe will teach me a lot about people and life. (Month 1)

According to his network contact log during the first week of school, Tom's language of choice was Spanish, even with his American friends. His social activities consisted of going out to <u>boliches</u> 'Argentine discos', lifting weights, getting a drink, sightseeing, and having meals with friends, who included Argentines, Mexicans, French, and North Americans. In Figure 6 it can be seen that Tom was using more Spanish than English.

Figure 6. Tom's Language Choice Over Time in Social Situations

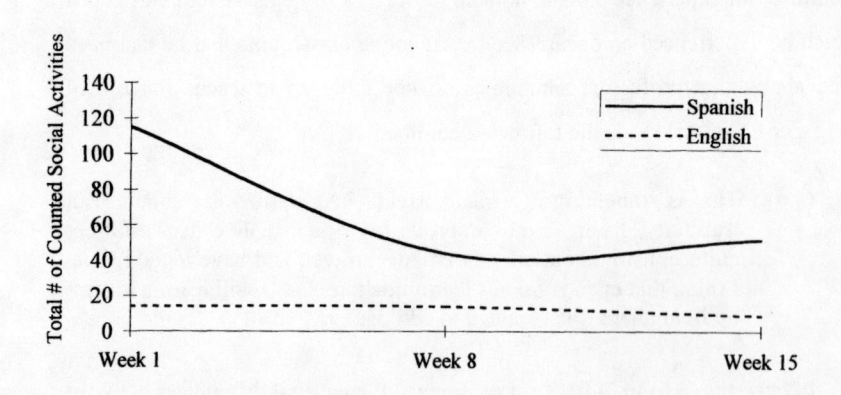

During his first month Tom chose to speak to everyone in Spanish, even his American fellow students. By the second month his use of Spanish decreased, which correlates with the fact that he started to have problems with his French roommate. He noted in his diary entries that the roommate frequently criticized US politics and current news. Tom found it difficult to stand up for his country and express his opinions and justifications for US actions in Spanish, so he switched to English. Since most of his time in the apartment was spent speaking or arguing with his roommate, as compared to when he lived with a host family whose members spoke to him only in Spanish, the drop in his use of Spanish can be explained. It must be noted that he still chose Spanish over English in social situations.

By his second month, Tom felt he had made improvement in his language acquisition, as noted in the first sentence of a diary entry,

> (4.11) "Well it makes [sic] three weeks that I have had classes. God, I am thinking in Spanish 'it makes' above."

When Spanish grammar and vocabulary structures begin to infiltrate a learner's English structures, it is usually seen as an accomplishment in learning a second language. It also reveals that he was speaking a substantial amount of Spanish.

Tom was also preoccupied with finding a volunteer job. Part of his academic credit abroad had to be obtained by volunteering in a certain sector of the Argentine society and writing a report about his experience with that position. Excerpt (4.12), taken from Tom's second month abroad, illustrates his frustration concerning his difficulty with finding a volunteer position in Buenos Aires and how he attributed his feelings to both the immediate situation and his other problems.

> (4.12) It just amazes me that it is this difficult to find a place to volunteer. In US there are so many opportunities [...]. Well, I now have some volunteer project to do. I am going to work in a church feeding the homeless, etc. [...]. I have been extremely frustrated and much of my anger was directed at Argentina. It seemed that no one wanted to help me find anything to do and that anyone that could have helped me was never around [...]. Many of my frustrations have come from tasks that should be so simple, but Latin America has chosen that it doesn't want to be that way [...]. I do feel a little homesick, but this is also because I have been so damn frustrated and upset lately [...]. (Month 2)

Tom blamed the fact that he could not find a volunteer position on a cultural characteristic that he seemed to attribute not only to Argentina, but to all of Latin America: that things cannot be simple. Tom's belief about the Latin American system suggests that the US system of accomplishing tasks is more efficient and effective than the Argentine system. In other words, he regarded the US as a country in which tasks are accomplished without as many problems.

The feeling of frustration that Tom felt was described in De Ley (1975) in his "stranger" theory. On arrival in a foreign country, routine activities may require intense mental effort; in this case, finding a place to work for free, something that requires very little effort in the US. Tom was frustrated with what he perceived as indifference to his needs as a study abroad student. According to De Ley, after feeling frustrated at the fact that common activities can be so difficult, the sojourner experiences fatigue and a growing feeling of meaninglessness, or "anomie." Victims of anomie react with anger and tend to reject the ways of their hosts.

Individuals can overcome anomie by locating themselves in their new environment. They can find places, institutions, work, and circles of acquaintances that allow them self-definition, and hence self-confirmation, in their new homes (pp. 837-838). Tom accomplished this hurdle by week 12 when he found himself incorporated into his new group of acquaintances made up of the volunteers. In (4.13), he recommends volunteer work to future students.

> (4.13) I have begun to not feel homesick again [...]. For a future note I think exchange students [...] ought to do something like this [volunteer] during their study abroad. I have met some really nice people my age [...] that are also helping out here. These people are more like really meeting people of the country as friends because lots of people we meet is because we are exchange students [...]. I really enjoyed chatting with the people, especially the other volunteers. (Month 3)

A more detailed account of Tom's social network activity during his five months abroad can be seen in Table 15.

TABLE 15. Tom's First and Second Order Zone Social Networks

SOPI rating	Month	1st order zone uniplex Argentine members	2nd order zone multiplex Argentine members
IM	1	7	
	2		
	3	9	
	4		
IH	5	9	(1) in progress

SOPI=Simulated Oral Proficiency Interview, IM=Intermediate Mid, IH = Intermediate High.

Figure 7. Tom's (X) First and Second Order Zone Social Networks

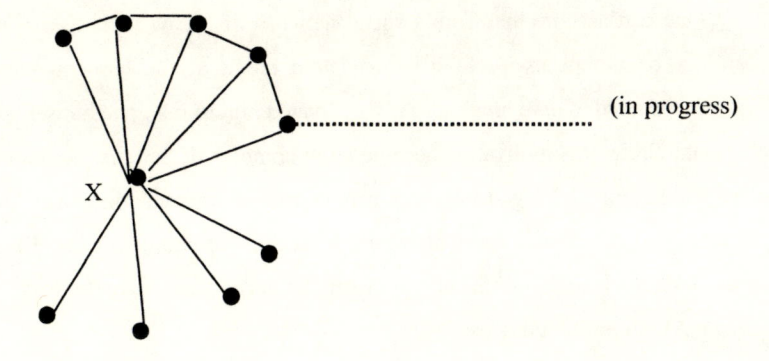

(in progress)

First Order Zone   Second Order Zone

As can be seen in Figure 7, during Tom's Month 1, the members of his uniplex first order zone represent his host family members and three study abroad administrators. These associations were uniplex since his role with them was as a guest with his family and as a new study abroad student to the administrators.

During the third month, Tom was no longer living with his host family and his contact with them decreased significantly. Instead, his social network during Month 3 consisted of five Argentines who volunteered at the church where he volunteered and four other Argentine acquaintances whom he had gone out with several times. By Month 5, Tom frequently had lunch with the group of five volunteers and began spending time with one Argentine girl, Romina, normally having lunch with her and talking to her on the phone. Romina represents the beginning of a social network extension from first order zone members, with whom he associated in a uniplex manner, to a second order zone. Romina alone cannot be considered part of a second order zone social network; only when Romina includes Tom in her circle of friends and frequent interactions with those members occur can the social network be considered multiplex. I can only speculate that this extension would have developed had Tom had more time to establish his relationship with Romina.

One can assume that Tom's social network of fellow volunteer workers began out of the necessity to gain academic credit at his home university. Although the need to earn credit initially motivated him to integrate himself into a new social circle, this motivation became more complex during the program. He gained and maintained friendships with people from another ethnolinguistic group he wanted to know better and with whom he wanted to communicate. In other words, Tom had an "investment" to learn the target language; to make and maintain Argentine friendships.

By Month 5, Tom had adapted to the Argentine social and academic system, demonstrated by his successful library research and also by his social network of Argentine volunteers. Although it may be the case that Tom adapted to the Argentine lifestyle, he indicates his belief in excerpt (4.14), taken from his fifth month diary entry, that the US culture dominates over the Argentine culture.

> (4.14) One major problem I see for this country is whether or not the people will have the training and knowledge to advance as they want. I think major changes need to be made to give the people greater access to the needed learning materials [...]. I am being critical but it is only because I think there is a lot of room for improvement. (Month 5)

This excerpt was written after Tom relayed the difficulty he experienced in obtaining articles in the library and getting simple tasks accomplished, which he stated was an impediment to the advancement of the Argentine people. Although Tom did not stop at the stage of anomie and did not give up trying to learn the language, he still shows a hegemonic attitude toward the Argentine culture by giving advice because "there is a lot of room for improvement." This excerpt shows that one can adapt to the culture without liking everything. Tom separated those things he did not like about the Argentine culture from his experience in learning about the culture.

The enduring presence of a hegemonic attitude was not an obstacle to Tom's acculturation, which may be an important step in the establishment of social networks. This acculturation was illustrated by the fact that Tom's social network grew to include a group of ten Argentines, the majority of whom were participants in his volunteer program.

Apart from his continuing hegemonic attitude toward Argentina, Tom's broad social network of Argentines, his measured positive attitude towards the host culture, and his high motivation to learn the language affected his second language development. We saw in the previous chapter that Tom showed development in linguistic accuracy with a positive slope of 3.92 and stopped struggling to create appropriate forms by his third month abroad. He relied on Intermediate High functions at the beginning of the program, using simple speech functions, and began to incorporate more advanced functions during his last month abroad. Tom's development in both linguistic accuracy and oral communication skills correlates to his positive attitude toward the culture, high motivation to learn the language, and the beginning extension of his social network with native speakers. His oral proficiency rating increased one level.

Mark's attitudes and social network

According to his interviews and his diary excerpts, Mark, who began at the Intermediate Low level and ended the program at Intermediate High, thought that he was fortunate to have Lucy as his host mother in Argentina. Lucy was a divorced woman who made sure there was plenty of food on the table accompanied by abundant conversation. Mark wrote, "I'm lucky to have such a cool host mother" and "Lucy is a pretty decent cook and she always makes so much, so I never go hungry." Lucy treated him like an important member of the household.

In his interviews, Mark made constant references to Lucy, Lucy's boyfriend, and Lucy's adult goddaughter, from whom he learned a great deal about Argentina's political history and culture. Table 16 illustrates Mark's social network distribution and diagramed in Figure 8.

TABLE 16. Mark's First and Second Order Zone Social Networks

SOPI rating	Month	1st order zone uniplex Argentine members	2nd order zone multiplex Argentine members
IL	1	1	3
	2		
	3	2	3
	4		
IH	5	2	3

SOPI=Simulated Oral Proficiency Interview, IL=Intermediate Low, IH=Intermediate High.

The member in Mark's Month 1 first order zone social network was Lucy, his host mother. She quickly introduced Mark to her boyfriend and her goddaughter, with whom he interacted at various levels such as study abroad student, political debater, and member of the household. These three people were solid components of his second order zone social network throughout the program.

The two other members of his first order zone were Argentine friends of his study abroad friends with whom he went out with in large groups.

Figure 8. Mark's (X) First and Second Order Zone Social Networks

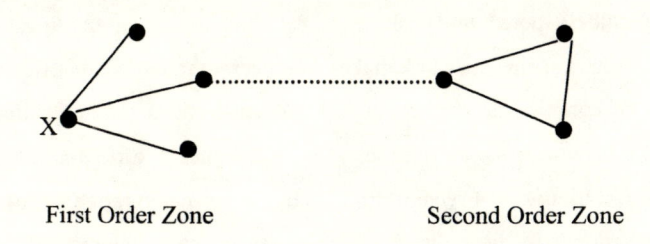

First Order Zone   Second Order Zone

Although the quality of Mark's host family was crucial to his social network, it must also be mentioned that his laidback personality and willingness to interact with his host family also played an important role in the building and maintenance of this network. Just because he had a friendly host mother did not automatically mean that she intended to include Mark in her social circle. Mark's personality and curiosity of the language and culture may have also been a crucial aspect in the building of his strong social network.

Mark's measured attitude toward his new host culture was positive throughout the study abroad program. His first-month diary entries are full of observations ranging from his progress with the language to nightlife and from physical aspects of the women of Buenos Aires to police corruption. Of the observations made during his second month, he made several neutral observations and one that indicated a personal negative opinion. This opinion is noted in excerpt (4.15), in which Mark describes his expectations of the architecture of Buenos Aires:

> (4.15) I really did not know what to expect about the city itself. But I was disappointed a little bit with the physical beauty of BA [Buenos Aires]. I thought there would be many more old style type buildings than there are. Instead the city is dominated by those god-awful apartment high rises [...]. I am lucky enough to live in

an old apartment building that has a little bit of personality. BA [Buenos Aires] is such a city of contrasts architecture-wise. (Month 2)

Although he wrote that the city is full of "those god-awful apartment high-rises" he quickly noted the positive aspect that he was living in a nice old building. In his conclusion, Mark makes an objective statement that Buenos Aires is "a city of contrasts architecture-wise." A learner in a state of culture shock generally does make such an observation immediately after finding negative aspects and Mark does not seem to fit into any of the acculturation stages. During his second month in the program, he was neither in a "honeymoon" stage in which he would praise everything he experienced or observed nor was he in a state of culture shock or stress. He was culturally and mentally open to any aspect of the new culture. This personal quality, along with his mellow personality, may have enabled him to take in aspects of the new culture easily. It should be noted that Mark frequently traveled within the US, an activity that may lend to his adaptation to new situations with great ease.

Excerpt (4.16), taken from his second month's diary entries, includes his expectations of "big-city" personalities following the previous observation in excerpt (4.15) of the building structures in Buenos Aires. Mark expected that the population of Buenos Aires would share the same characteristics as those of big cities in the US.

(4.16) For such a big city the people in BA [Buenos Aires] don't seem to have that aloof, keep-to-yourself attitude that I normally equate with cities. What I mean is, I have seen on more than one occasion people stopping to talk to homeless (what few there are). One time I saw a lady chase down a little kid who was begging and give him an alfajor ['chocolate wafer'] while waiting in line for a movie [...]. Another time I saw this guy who was apparently homeless sitting in a doorway and bawling his eyes out. During the 30 minutes he sat there there must have been 7 or 8 people who stopped to console him [...]. Things like that strike me as peculiar in such a large city. (Month 2)

It is clear that Mark chose to write about positive aspects of what he perceived to be an element of Argentine culture. As he stated in excerpt (4.15), he did not know what to expect from Buenos Aires before arriving with respect to the physical beauty of the city or the people. He did have a preconception that the city would have older buildings and that the people would be "aloof" just like the stereotypical inhabitants of large cities in the US. Mark did not criticize the elements in his new host country; in fact, he stated that the attention of the porteños paid to the downtrodden, poor people was better than that of US urban residents.

The following excerpt (4.17), taken from his fourth month diary entry, was tallied as one of several instances indicating Mark's overall positive attitude toward his study abroad experience in Argentina.

> (4.17) I am glad to be here because I am here during a point in Argentine history where they are trying desperately to assert themselves in the Western World [...]. It appears as though the city is just starting to enjoy itself after the military rule [...]. I believe that I have a unique opportunity in order to gain a perspective on a city trying to establish its own identity. (Month 4)

Mark was very appreciative to be in Buenos Aires and acknowledged the benefit of being abroad, which he repeated several times in his diary entries and informal interviews. As mentioned in Chapter 2, his measured positive attitude translated to his high motivational orientation to learn the language. Excerpts such as (4.18), taken from his fifth month diary entries, also evidence Mark's high motivational orientation to acquire Spanish.

> (4.18) Sometimes I am satisfied with the level that I have reached, but the majority of the time I'm not. That is why I am staying a year. I just don't want my Spanish to be passable, I want it to be where I think in Spanish and can communicate just as effectively as in English. Bueno, vamos a ver. (Month 5)

According to his network contact log, Mark spent a great deal of time talking with Lucy and her friends. In fact, they offered most of the information on pre- and post-military rule in Argentina. It must be noted that Mark's social network did consist of American students and other Argentines with whom he attended soccer games, horse races, polo games, and bar outings. Although he was motivated to be in Argentina to learn the language and had a positive attitude toward the host culture, his language choice in social situations tended to be English over Spanish as seen in Figure 9.

Figure 9. Mark's Language Choice Over Time in Social Situations

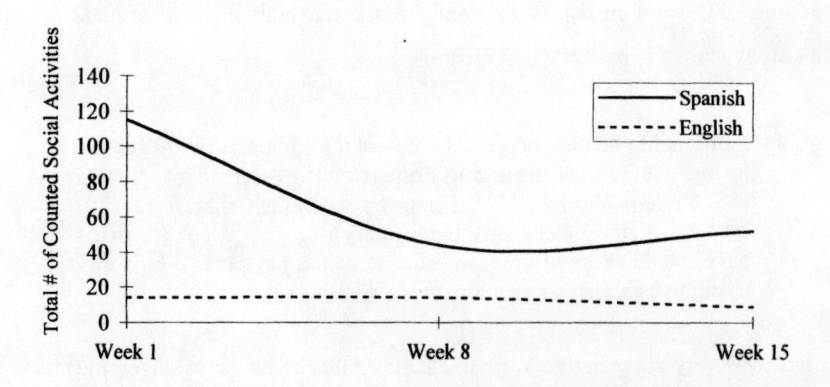

After Week 8, however, this language choice changed to a slight preference for Spanish over English when he was engaged in social situations.

Mark's most pressing concern throughout his study abroad experience was his fear of not improving past an Intermediate proficiency level at the end of the program. He did not want his Spanish to be mediocre; he wanted to think in Spanish and communicate as effectively in Spanish as he did in English. He was enthusiastic when he communicated for long periods of time with Argentines in noisy places: "My Spanish must be doing something right because it is certainly not my good looks that get me by with the local girls." This comment is also an indicator of a possible motivation, or even "investment", to want to communicate effectively in Spanish.

Mark maintained a positive attitude toward the culture and had high motivation to learn Spanish. That positive characteristic, along with the strong membership of his host mother and her friends in his social network, allowed for Mark to be in situations in which he practiced more advanced speech functions. This factor in turn allowed for his development of oral communication skills and linguistic accuracy, discussed in Chapter 3. Mark's overall development in linguistic accuracy at the end of the program was positive, $\beta = 2.51$. The aspects of his oral communication skills that showed development were fluency and functions attempted. Throughout the semester Mark's speech consisted of using less difficult functions and, by Months 3 and 4, more difficult ones appeared in his narratives. By the end of the program, Mark produced more words per response, had fewer pauses in his speech samples, and decreased in the number of times he struggled with the language. All these factors played a role in Mark's oral skills development, which started at an Intermediate Low level at the beginning of the program and ended at an Intermediate High level, jumping two levels. In fact, Mark's initial decision was to stay for only one semester in Argentina. Because of his strong social network and his desire for more improvement in his communication skills, Mark decided to continue in the program for the remainder of the academic year.

Sam's attitudes and social network

Sam, whose pre- and post-program SOPI scores were Intermediate Mid and Intermediate High, respectively, lived in an apartment with three other exchange students, two North Americans and a Mexican, with whom he reported to speak both Spanish and English. He had traveled throughout South America for a several weeks before actually starting the program in Buenos Aires.

During his first week in Buenos Aires, his diary entry made reference only to his perceived progress in the acquisition of the language and to some difficulties he had in understanding Argentine colloquialisms. By Week 5, his diary entry consisted of a lengthy discussion of his experience with corruption in Buenos Aires and various situations in which corruption occurs. He wrote at length on this topic in excerpt (4.19), in which he included numerous criticisms about Argentines.

> (4.19) Corruption here is quite rampant [...]. Somebody told me that the Policia Federal had to take cuts from whores, black market people, etc. to even be able to operate. The night watchman in our apartment building gets bribed by husbands who sneak whores into the building. And Menem calls this a First World country [...]. Argentines seem to think that they are the shit of South America for some reason. Wealthy ones especially [...]. There cannot be enough jobs out there that pay enough to give people the lifestyles that they are living currently [...]. Maybe they are all surviving by bribing the next person down the line with that person doing the same [...]. I read an article in a newspaper here that made some statement about the fact that God was Argentine. Whatever. (Month 2)

His reference to the fact that the former President of Argentina, Carlos Saúl Menem, "calls this [Argentina] a First World country" is, in fact, sarcastic. He questions how Argentina could belong to the First World when there is corruption and bribery taking place in a range of occupations, from the police force to ordinary businesses. One can only assume that he is comparing this activity to what he believes does not occur in the US, a "First World" country. Sam reinforces his perception of the hegemony of the US over Argentina through derogatory remarks about cultural differences directed towards the Argentine mentality. In his view, the North American society is morally superior to that of the Argentines.

By Week 8, Sam's diary entry focuses on a different yet important aspect of the Buenos Aires lifestyle during the time of the investigation: cellular phones.

Because cellular phone companies were fiercely competing to offer the best deal to the consumer, the cost of buying and maintaining a cellular phone in Buenos Aires had become quite low and it was now very practical to own one. It was quite common to see people talking on a cellular phone while using public transportation or even riding a bicycle (a fad that had yet to hit the U.S.). Sam concentrates on the fact that the use of these cell phones is sometimes annoying and foolish.

> (4.20) Argentines are big on their cellular phones. So big that it has reached the point of being obnoxiously annoying [...]. I have seen people in the gym stop right in the middle of sets to answer their phone, which they next spend 10 minutes talking on and most incredible motorcyclists in the middle of 9 de Julio pull over to answer a call. Now what the hell can be that important? [...] I cannot yet figure out why some people (damn near every Argentine) needs to be reachable at all times. They must think that it makes them look important or something. (Month 2)

Sam shows resentment and even anger toward these Argentines when he asks what can be so important to be on the phone all the time and comments that the Argentines think the cell phone makes them look important. He includes all Argentines in his criticism, unable to separate his annoyance of phone carriers from the porteño culture. It is not surprising that, due to his belief of the cultural immorality and his annoyance at Argentina, his social network during the first weeks of this study consisted of other study abroad learners going through the same situation.

At this point in the program Sam's language choice while in social situations was slightly more Spanish than English, seen in Figure 10. By the middle of the program to the end of his stay abroad, Sam self-reported that he spoke more English than Spanish in social situations. The increase in Sam's use of English correlates with the tone of his diary entries, which became more critical of the host culture as time went on.

Figure 10. Sam's Language Choice Over Time in Social Situations

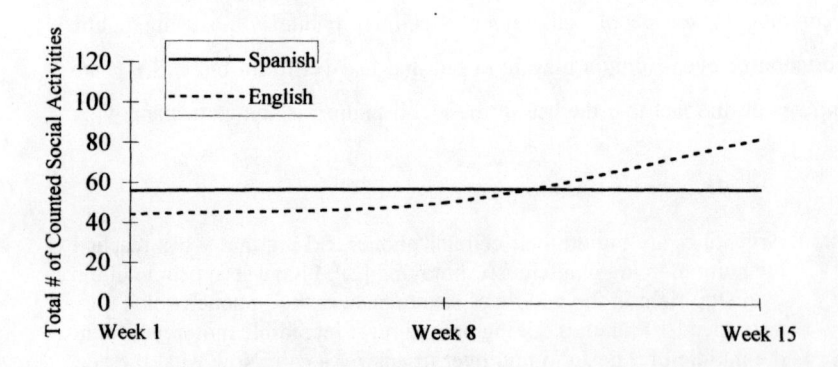

[Chart: Total # of Counted Social Activities vs. Week 1, Week 8, Week 15. Spanish (solid line) stays around 55-60; English (dashed line) starts around 40 and rises to about 80 by Week 15.]

By the end of the study abroad program, the low opinion that Sam had for Argentines, especially for male Argentines, was quite evident, as can be seen in excerpt (4.21) taken from a diary entry during his fourteenth week abroad.

(4.21) If you think that Argentine men are bad with women when they are sober (which they are) then they really are something to see when drunk [...]. No girl whatsoever can leave a boliche ['night-club'] without getting hit on several times. It gets rather disgusting after awhile [...]. And if you are a hot woman who goes to one, get ready for a long night full of annoying prides. You shoot down one guy and five others step forward to take his place, all of them perfectly confident that they are the man of your dreams (you just do not know it yet). And refuse to take no for an answer. (Month 3)

Sam was disgusted by the disregard that Argentine men seemed to show toward women. Throughout the duration of the program, it was shown through his diary entries that Sam regarded Argentine men as corrupt, foolish, and disrespectful towards women. These entries outnumbered his positive remarks about the host culture, which translated to a low motivation to learn the language. This perception may explain why his social network of Argentine acquaintances was limited to three to four people (two men and two women) throughout his study abroad experience, which is shown in Table 17 and diagramed in Figure 11.

TABLE 17. Sam's First and Second Order Zone Social Networks

SOPI rating	Month	1st order zone uniplex Argentine members	2nd order zone multiplex Argentine members
IM	1	3	
	2		
	3	4	
	4		
IH	5	3	

SOPI=Simulated Oral Proficiency Interview, IM=Intermediate Mid, IH = Intermediate High.

Figure 11. Sam's (X) First and Second Order Zone Social Networks

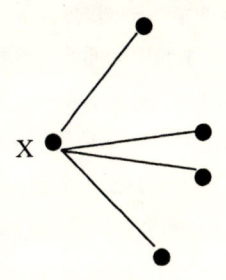

First Order Zone   Second Order Zone

Those who were part of Sam's first order zone network during Month 1 were the two program organizers and his Spanish grammar teacher in Buenos Aires. By Months 3 and 5 his social network included one program organizer and two to three Argentines with whom he frequently went out with in large groups of study abroad students. He showed no indication of extending this first order zone uniplex relationship to a multiplex one with any of the members. Sam's lack of "investment" to learn the target language, his negative attitude toward the host culture, and low motivation hindered him from building significant social networks with Argentines. Sam interacted with few Argentines and socialized within large group settings with other study abroad students. His social practices rarely gave him an opportunity to talk about topics at length, in which he may have been able to practice more advanced speech functions.

In the previous chapter, the data concerning the development of Sam's linguistic accuracy and oral communication skills in Spanish indicate improvement, but only in linguistic accuracy, which was not attributed to his social networks. This pattern could be due to the fact that when Sam produced his highly accurate utterances, they were brief and unelaborated. He produced accurate grammar in his brief responses and avoided elaboration where possible linguistic difficulties could arise. During his interviews, Sam was unable to produce speech samples that were of moderate quantity or even of paragraph length, two features that are characteristic of Advanced level speakers. He tended to socialize with other study abroad learners in English and, according to his network contact log, he did speak in Spanish but usually in large groups of people. Large group conversations probably did not allow Sam the opportunity to practice more detailed speech functions. As was noted in Chapter 3, Sam's interviews were characterized by his focus on the production of accurate grammar and functions lacking in content and detail.

Sam's negative attitude toward the host culture and low motivation to learn the second language hindered him from building significant social networks with Argentines. Considering Sam's few opportunities to practice Spanish with native speakers, his preference to use English in social situations as the semester went on, his negative attitude towards the people of the host culture, and low motivation, how can his development in oral ability be explained? In offering a possible reason for Sam's jump in proficiency levels from Intermediate Mid to Intermediate High, we must look at an element from Sam's profile: he read a lot of Argentine newspapers. Although Sam may not have participated in many conversational interactions with Argentines, explaining the lack of development in his use of more advanced functions, he may have been exposed to different kinds of discourse in reading, possibly explaining his development in linguistic accuracy. Through this activity, he may have been exposed to discourse that enabled him to develop certain aspects in his speech, such as semi-organization and connectedness, use of appropriate vocabulary, and accuracy of grammar.

Jennifer's attitudes and social network

Jennifer, whose pre- and post-program SOPI ratings were both Intermediate Mid, showed motivation in her pre-program questionnaire to be part of the study abroad program. Her pre-program expectation was to become competent in the language. She was an instrumentally motivated learner as revealed in her desire to incorporate Spanish in her future career of agriculture.

During her first month, Jennifer maintained a very positive attitude in her diary entries as seen in excerpt (4.22), in which she discusses the members of her social network at the time.

> (4.22) I'm in a class in agronomy and all of the other students except one are male and most are gauchos. What was interesting to me was their behavior in class. They acted very macho by putting their feet up on the desk [...]. Also, they passed mate ['tea'] back and forth throughout the class, even the teacher asked to have a few cups. Here they are very relaxed about class times [...]. I went to an asado ['barbeque'] last week [with classmates][...]. They were very hospitable and cooked very well [...]. The boys that I went with are so much more accommodating than American boys are. They would open doors for me, accompany me to where I was going and make certain that I was comfortable. (Month 1)

Jennifer's diary entry focuses on practices that do not happen in the US but seem to indicate her belief that they should exist: relaxation in the classroom, camaraderie with the instructor, and gentlemanly behavior of 18-year-old men.

These descriptions were tallied as positive attitudes toward the host culture but Jennifer's social attitude quickly changed when in the same diary entry she posits the advantage of the US culture over that of Argentina, as seen in excerpt (4.23):

> (4.23) When I am running in the park alone, the men playing soccer often stop and look and yell things at me. That would never happen in the US I think it stems from arrogance because they think that all women want to impress them. (Month 1)

Along with feeling the euphoria of being in a new country that usually occurs upon arrival, according to Bennett's (1986) sociological research on acculturation, Jennifer showed signs of the second stage of ethnocentrism during the first month in that she recognized the reality of cultural differences but at times preserved the hegemony of her culture over the target culture.

Jennifer's initial signs of positive attitude disappeared within the initial week of her stay abroad as noted in her diary entries. Jennifer experienced an unpleasant first month because she was living with a single woman who treated Jennifer like a tenant in a very small apartment. She gave her a key and had little or no contact with her. Since Jennifer expected to have more contact with her host family, she complained to the program director and, after rejecting another family comprised of only a husband and wife, she finally decided to live with a four-member family that included two children. Her social network during Month 1, which can be seen in Table 18 and diagramed in Figure 12, consisted of her host family and three Argentine classmates with whom she spoke Spanish.

Following these initial weeks in Argentina, Jennifer's social network of Argentines decreased to include only her host family and her American friend and remained this way throughout the duration of her stay abroad.

TABLE 18. Jennifer's First and Second Order Zone Social Networks

SOPI rating	Month	1st order zone uniplex Argentine members	2nd order zone multiplex Argentine members
IM	1	8	
	2		
	3	4	
	4		
IM	5	4	

SOPI=Simulated Oral Proficiency Interview, IM=Intermediate Mid.

Figure 12. Jennifer's (X) First and Second Order Zone Social Networks

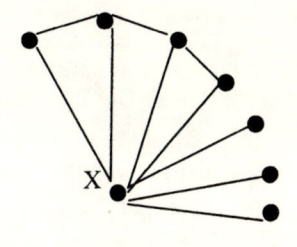

First Order Zone   Second Order Zone

With her host family, she usually had breakfast or a cup of coffee during the day. Most often she would play with the children or watch television with them in Spanish. She also socialized on a regular basis with English-speaking people. Such social activities would include going out or having dinner with them. In her diary entries, Jennifer indicated in her third week diary entry that her small social network with Argentines had influenced her progress in acquiring the target language (4.24).

> (4.24) I am very frustrated trying to speak [Spanish] because I am timid about my pronunciation. It is also hard to speak when the majority of the people that I have talked to speak English. (Month 1)

A week later, during her fourth week abroad, Jennifer also began to be critical of the Argentines' mannerisms and lifestyles. In excerpt (4.25), Jennifer comments on the political incorrectness of pointing out and directly commenting on one's physical appearance, especially concerning the topic of weight.

> (4.25) I have noticed that Argentine men are not at all shy about telling a girl she is fat. Several times I have been walking on the street or with friends and someone has pointed out the fact that I am not stick thin. I can't imagine being an Argentine woman and putting up with that [...]. (Month 1)

In another excerpt during the same week, she criticizes her host family's lack of certain values as compared to those values that she believes exist in the US:

> (4.26) I don't think my family (in Argentina) values education as much as in the US. The children only go to school for half days and often just don't go because they've overslept. (Month 1)

And during her fifth week abroad, she comments on the lack of friendliness in Argentine stores, something that she believes rarely happens in the US:

> (4.27) Also it seems that people in stores are ruder than in the States. If they don't carry what you want they don't apologize or suggest another store, they just say they don't have it. (Month 2)

By Month 3, a further deterioration can be seen in Jennifer's attitude toward the host culture. To her critical attitude she has added defeat.

> (4.28) I use the computer lab quite often and notice that the Argentine students are very loud and disrespectful. I think many of the other [American] students (not just me) have discovered that Argentines tend to be two faced. They will make promises and then not follow through [...]. I am really ready to go home. I think I have given up on this language. I don't feel very welcome in Argentina and have given up trying to make or keep Argentine friends. I am

very frustrated because there are many cultural things that bother me but I can't say anything because I don't want to offend anyone. (Month 3)

Excerpt (4.28) revealed that Jennifer felt isolated and separated from the new Argentine culture. She even commented the following during her fourth informal interview:

(4.29) Me siento que...yo no tengo un, un parte de esta cultura y...estoy harta de, estoy tratando de conseguir un, un lugar en este...cultura, pero no hay. (Month 4)

I feel that...I do not have a part in this culture and ...I am fed up with trying to find a place in this...culture, but there is not [any place].

This overall negative attitude, which is translated to her low motivation to learn the language, is also evidenced by the fact that halfway through the semester, her social network of Argentine friends consisted of only her host family. According to her network contact log, by this time she was spending the majority of her time with an American friend, going to movies, doing exercise, and traveling together. Note in Figure 13 how the dwindling size of her social network corresponded to the amount of Spanish she spoke.

Although she reported that she spoke more Spanish than English in social situations, she participated in fewer activities and not only spoke less Spanish than during her first weeks abroad, but English as well (see Figure 8). A possible explanation for Jennifer's self-report data is that the it was easier for her to remember instances when she spoke Spanish and therefore tally it. When she was in Spanish social situations, she was with the children of the household or other Argentine staff or faculty of the study abroad program, in which the social interaction was not consequential. That is, interaction with these people may have not have involved extended discourse but was tallied as an social interaction nonetheless.

Figure 13. Jennifer's Language Choice Over Time in Social Situations

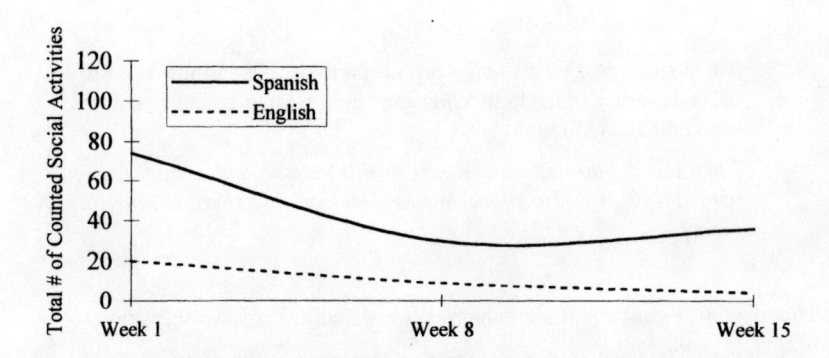

The sense of isolation that Jennifer felt from the Argentine community overcame her. "Many cultural things" bothered her and instead of minimizing the cultural differences to adapt to the environment she maximized her time with what she was familiar with, American friendships and the English language. She included in her fourth informal interview an explanation of why she had difficulty making friends, seen in excerpt (4.30).

> (4.30) La cultura argentina es…siempre quieren ser europeano y son muy, muy superficial y…si, si una chica no tiene…nada acá o no tiene mucha plata o…algo, algo para darles, ella no es nada. (Month 4)
>
> *The Argentine culture is…they always want to be European and they are very, very superficial and…if a girl does not have…anything here o does not have a lot of money or…something to give them, she is nothing.*

The establishment of social networks in a new environment cannot be accomplished without advancement of the learner's cultural awareness and the study abroad participant must reach a state of ethnorelativism before this occurs (Bennett, 1986, p. 46). Jennifer stagnated in the first of six stages towards reaching this state of ethnorelativism, never gaining cultural awareness and finally giving up altogether on making Argentine friends.

In Chapter 3, it was shown that, although Jennifer had a positive degree of development in linguistic accuracy, it was minimal. There was no progress in her overall oral ability, which was illustrated in the extreme brevity of the quantity of speech in her interviews. Jennifer also relied solely on the use of the present tense regardless of the form needed, which is partially explained by the fact that she did not have the opportunity to practice narrating in the past in Spanish. Her social network consisted of the members of her host family; most of her time she did not talk to the adults but rather to the children. She expressed in her diary that when she did have contact with the children, she usually played with them and at times read them children's books. I do not know enough to say which elements caused Jennifer's failure to acquire a past tense or if a single factor played a part in her lack of development in oral ability. One reason could have been that Jennifer did not seek opportunities in which she could practice more advanced conversational strategies, such as discussing topics of current public or personal interest. In addition, the negative attitude that she had toward the host culture and low motivation to learn the language hindered her from including more Argentines in her social network, lacking any "investment" to learn the target language.

Jennifer did not seek opportunities in which she could practice more advanced conversational strategies such as discussing topics of current public or personal interest. Consequently, as seen in Chapter 3, her speech functions were reduced to scattered instances of simple speech production. Her utterance lengths were also the shortest of all the learners in this study. In addition, the negative attitude that she had toward the host culture and low to learn the language hindered her from including more Argentines in her social network with whom she would have been able to practice more advanced functions.

Summary

Providing an inside look at the learners' thoughts and opinions toward the new host cultural experiences, an analysis of the breadth of their social networks through network contact logs indicated that the positive or negative aspects of their thoughts and opinions played a role in their desire and drive to build a new social network. It was shown that those students who were involved in social networks had a tendency to implement more advanced functions such as narrating with elaboration and explicitness of description and telling a story in such a way that the story recipients understood the "point".

The students with stronger social networks were able to practice those functions with more frequency than those with a weak social network, which resulted in a significant development in their oral communication skills. It must also be noted that the learners' attitudes toward the host culture usually corresponded to their language choice in social situations

Chapter 5
CONCLUDING REMARKS

> *"I'm glad I did it [study abroad] but I wish it would have been easier to meet people from [the] University, so we can feel more like a part of the community."* -Tom

To date, second language acquisition research has examined some aspects of how learners' oral ability improves during a study abroad program, but few studies have addressed the changes of specific linguistic aspects. As surveyed in the Introduction, research shows that the study abroad environment is beneficial to the acquisition of the target language, especially in improvement of oral production ability (Brecht, Davidson, & Ginsberg, 1993; Carroll, 1967; Freed, 1990a, 1990b, 1995b; Howard, 2001; Isabelli, 2003; Kaplan, 1989; Lennon, 1990b; Liskin-Gasparro & Urdaneta, 1995; Milleret, 1990; Polanyi, 1995).

Studies that break down the components of "oral production ability" come to similar conclusions, such as: increased narrative abilities and semantic density of words (Collentine, 2004); vocabulary acquisition (Milton & Meara, 1995), phonology (Díaz-Campos, 2004), fluency as measured by aspects such as flow and quantity of speech (DeKeyser, 1991; Freed, 1995b; Freed, Segalowitz & Dewey, 2004; Lafford, 1995; Segalowitz & Freed, 2004; Towell, Hawkins, & Bazergui, 1996); and, ability to carry out oral ability (Lafford, 2004). But Freed, Segalowitz, and Dewey (2004) add that the domestic immersion group showed greater fluency than the study abroad group and Lafford (1995) evidences that at home students acquire more communicative strategies than the study abroad groups. But she adds that, "study abroad speakers find out that it is more efficient to try to communicate one's ideas quickly (although somewhat imperfectly) in order to accomplish the goal at hand" while classroom learners ... do not experience the same kind of pragmatic pressure to get the meaning across" (p. 111).

Several studies evidence that the study abroad context is beneficial to the development of specific language structures (Howard 2001; Lennon 1990b; Ryan & Lafford 1992) whereas others have come to contradictory conclusions (Collentine, 2004; Freed 1995a; Moehle 1984; Möhle & Raupach 1983; Raupach 1983, 1984; Regan 1995). Other studies indicate that study abroad does not necessarily predict development in oral ability (DeKeyser, 1991; Huebner, 1995). Research collected throughout the immersion process that shows gains in oral ability does not detail what linguistic aspects do improve (Lapkin, Hart, & Swain, 1995).

Studies carried out to investigate the role that social interaction plays in language acquisition have also produced contradictory conclusions, some providing evidence that suggests that informal contact does not necessarily enhance acquisition (DeKeyser 1991; Frank 1997; Freed, 1990b; Krashen et al., 1974; Krashen & Seliger, 1976; Pellegrino 1998; Segalowitz & Freed, 2004; Spada, 1985, 1986; Wilkinson 1997, 1998) and may even hinder it (Higgs & Clifford, 1982). Yet other studies conclude that interaction has an impact on the acquisition of sociolinguistic and sociocultural knowledge (Lafford, 1995; Lapkin, Hart, & Swain, 1995; Marriot, 1995; Regan, 1995; Siegal, 1995).

As can be seen, there are inconsistencies in the research since claims are made based on different acquisition aspects, distinct amounts of time spent abroad and the type of interaction between learners and native speakers is not specified, making it difficult to generalize across studies of study abroad experiences and gains. One of the goals of this study was to describe and account for the regularities and the variations in the social attitudes of language learners in the study abroad context. Data collected through ethnographic interviews and journals revealed that some learners remained bound to their own culture while others did not.

The well known SOPI allowed me to obtain participants' ratings of proficiency. I enhanced this with a speech corpus created from informal interviews, which I analyzed for development of linguistic accuracy and oral communication skills. In doing so, I came across for examples that illustrated qualities that are used to constitute the SOPI ratings of a more advanced speaker, such as: meshing the descriptive background with the sequential recounting of events, providing the sensorial richness and explicitness of description, and providing cohesive and coherent arguments in support of that opinion. This study then explored the hypothesis that development of linguistic accuracy and oral communication skills correlates with the learners' motivation and attitude toward the host culture and the breadth of their social networks. Other related objectives of the study were to: (1) attain a more complete understanding of what needs to be accomplished by the language learner to take full advantage of being in the study abroad environment and enhance language skills; and (2) explore factors that the study abroad context offers the learners that can stimulate the acquisition process, such as opportunities to change perceptions of cultural awareness and to interact with various native speakers.

Findings

What kind of development is seen in the learners' linguistic accuracy in Spanish while abroad?

The development of linguistic accuracy in the aspects studied for the five participants was generally positive and gradual. Some of the learners in this investigation showed much backsliding in their development of linguistic accuracy through the five-month period. Few students showed a steady increase with little to no interlanguage backsliding. The amount of backsliding that appeared in the learners' interviews reflects a reformulation of the learners' hypotheses about grammar rules of second language knowledge. Although this study did not compare the study abroad group with other types of foreign language study environments within other time frames other than the semester abroad, a direction for more study is needed to show that the more time that the learners spent abroad, the more time they had access to comprehensible input and were able to build on their linguistic knowledge of more advanced speech functions with the native speakers; thus, a development in accuracy is seen in their oral production. Isabelli (2004) found similar conclusions in that the acquisition of the lesser salient and more abstract feature, that-*trace*, is seen after 4 months.

Calculating a correlation only on the increase of linguistic development and frequency of social interaction was not and should not be done because it would draw superficial conclusions that the frequency of participation in social interactions leads to gains in linguistic development, failing to relate the whole story behind the acquisition process. We must take into consideration the learners that already show a high degree of accuracy at the beginning of the program, such as Stan, who will not have as much room for improvement as those who enter the program with a lower rate of linguistic accuracy, such as Mark. Both Mark and Stan had extensive interaction in social networks but Mark showed more development in linguistic accuracy than Stan because he began at a lower proficiency level.

Overall, most development in linguistic accuracy was seen in tense selection, while gender-number and subject-verb agreement showed slight development. The difficulties that the learners had in tense selection in the earlier interviews were attributed mostly to use of the present tense when a past tense was required.[17] Distinguishing aspect proved more difficult for the learners, a phenomenon that has been frequently noted in research (Andersen, 1990; Breiner-Sanders, et al., 2000; Terrell & Salgués de Cargill, 1979).

The problems that the learners showed with accurate aspect selection may be accounted for by the possibility that when the learners attend to comprehensible input in the host environment, they misperceive the distribution of a particular form. This misperception may lead to the inappropriate use of a particular morphological form, as explained by Andersen's (1990) Distributional Bias Principle. Since this study did not carry out this type of analysis, I cannot make this claim but offer it only as a possibility for future investigation.

What kind of development is seen in the learners' oral communication skills in Spanish while abroad?

I have learned that development in the learners' oral communication skills in communicating advanced level speech functions is one of the more complex aspects of language acquisition in which different factors, such as personality and confidence, play a role in the variability of learner development. The oral communication skills that are most often developed and practiced in a one-semester study abroad program are mostly those corresponding to a speaker that is characterized as having emerging evidence of connected discourse, particularly for simple narration and description, but errors are evident. This suggests that another semester abroad may bring the learner to acquire the ability to narrate and describe with some detail with the ability to handle past, present, and future verbs well, and make few agreement errors. Characteristics of a more experienced speaker of a language include high linguistic accuracy, the ability to state and support opinions and to give detailed descriptions instead of identifying discrete

---

[17]Alternation between the past tense and the historical present in order to draw the listener's attention to certain events and serve as an internal evaluation was not counted as an error of appropriateness of present versus past tense accuracy.

elements, and to tell a story instead of listing occurrences. A closer intimacy with members of a larger social network would seem to allow for more practice of advanced functions, since one does not usually give elaborate descriptions, narrations, and evaluations to those that one does not know well.

The learners' small overall development of the more advanced narrative functions correlates with the learners' small overall development in accuracy of aspect selection. Individual development was seen only in two learners, one of who (Stan) made a definite switch from using simple speech functions in his interviews to more detailed ones by the third month. The other (Tom) started to implement the more advanced speech functions during his last month abroad. The remaining three learners (Mark, Sam, and Jennifer) stayed constant throughout the program with the implementation of Intermediate speech functions. Collentine (2004) also found that despite the fact the study abroad students in his study did not make significant improvements in accuracy, their ability to produce narrative past-tense markers increased. Although Collentine defines and measures the development of narrative discourse a bit differently than I do in this study, it evidences a direction to develop in future research.

In a one-semester abroad experience, this area of oral communication skills is just becoming developed; more interaction time is needed abroad for learners to practice and learn to use the more advanced speech functions; that is, if motivation is high and their use of English decreases. This conclusion is derived from an analysis of the social network data for first and second order zone membership (Milroy, 1987) as discussed in Chapter 1. Briefly, a first order zone membership for study abroad learners is usually uniplex; the learner X interacts with each person in the network in only one capacity. A preferred second order zone social network is one in which a learner enters the social network of one of the members of his first order zone in which interaction is of a multiplex relationship. The two learners in this study that interacted in a multiplex second order zone social network were the only two that showed significant development in their speech functions. In their social network, they maintained a link from their uniplex first order zone, which consisted of Argentine acquaintances that did not know each other, to their multiplex second order, which consisted of a family or colleagues in a church group who did know each other.

This second order zone was the only way that the study abroad learners could interact in a "real" social network, meaning that the network did not consist only of acquaintances, none of who interacted with each other. Rather, the learners became part of a closed, multiplex network where opportunities to observe and participate in prolonged interaction was increased, giving them the opportunity to practice speech functions beyond that of supplying the superficial information. They were in social situations as a friend, and as such they were asked to embellish descriptions or felt obligated to give more evaluative comments so that their stories became a valued exchange to reinforce their friendship.

Quantity and flow of speech (Freed, 1995b; Freed, Segalowitz, & Dewey, 2004; Segalowitz & Freed, 2004) were the elements of the learners' overall oral communication skills that showed most development over the five-month study abroad period. Although the quantity and flow varied greatly among the learners, all but Sam showed an increase in quantity. Their speech at the end of the program had more flow with only occasional hesitations as compared to the beginning when there were intermittent hesitations throughout the interviews. Lafford (1995) comes to similar conclusions, "it is obvious that the study abroad groups evidence more facility with the language (fewer pauses while groping for words, shorter pauses, a faster rate of speed of their speech, etc.)" (p. 111). Also, Collentine (2004) states that the study abroad group in his study "increased its fluency over the treatment period, generating significantly more words on the posttest than on the pretest" (p. 235).

What is interesting to note is that three of the learners, except Stan and Sam, struggled to create appropriate forms in the first two interviews, but by the third interview and on, no struggle was seen. Stan was already at an Intermediate High level at the beginning of the program and was confident with his verb forms; therefore, he had no difficulties in expression and no groping for language, or "communication gap" (Lafford, 2004) was seen. On the other hand, Sam who also showed no struggling with accuracy throughout the program, focused greatly and worked to produce accurate forms during his interviews as evidenced by his high accuracy rate but brief, unelaborated responses.

Lafford (2004) evidenced that the study abroad context, as well as the at home one, "facilitated to some degree those learners' abilities to carry out communicative interaction in the L2 with fewer communication gaps at the end of the treatment period than at the beginning of the semester" (p. 212). The concept of *communication gap* is operationalized in her study as an interruption in the normal flow of conversational interaction between the speaker and interlocutor due to a breakdown in communication. One of Lafford's correlations indicate that fewer communication gaps were evidenced in more advanced speakers, such as Sam in the study, due to the lack of communication strategies (strategies used by second language learners in a conscious attempt to bridge a perceived communication gap) used.

The conclusions here also corroborate with those of Towell, Hawkins, and Bazergui (1996). As a result of a period of residence abroad, advanced learners of Spanish show a quantitative reduction in the amount of pausing they do and an increase in the length and complexity of linguistic units. The authors' conclusions suggest, "that what has changed is the rapidity with which syntactic and discourse knowledge can be accessed for on-line speech production" (p. 113). In other words, "A core feature of development in advanced L2 learners therefore seems to be the conversion of linguistic knowledge already acquired into rapidly-usable on-line 'productions' (p. 113). In addition, the data here supports conclusions of other research that the opportunities that the learners used to interact with the native speakers in their social networks allowed them to notice any gaps between their level of second language knowledge and the target language (their interlanguage) and to modify existing second language knowledge (Gass & Varonis, 1994; Lightbown, 1985). The learners used scaffolding strategies with their interactants (Donato, 1994; Lantolf & Appel, 1994; Vygotsky, 1978), which allowed them to build a repertoire of discourse skills. Through practice their interlanguage became somewhat restructured.

What individual factors (such as motivation, contact with host culture outside of the classroom, attitudes towards the host culture) enter into the success of development?

Why is it that Stan showed development in his linguistic and oral communication skills whereas Jennifer did not progress? Of course, these two participants represent the extremes in this study but, nonetheless, these questions are reasonable to ask. There are many intrinsic factors, such as different language learning strategies, extrovertedness, motivation, and attitude that influence the acquisition process, many of which cannot be controlled or even measured in such a study. Factors that have been widely studied and shown to have an effect on second language acquisition, as mentioned in the Introduction, are those of motivation and interaction. The influence of social networks has not been researched in second language acquisition.

The motivation of the learner towards learning the target language does affect the language learning process. It was shown that the learners with high motivation (Stan, Mark, and Tom), as opposed to low motivation (Jennifer and Sam) developed more extensive social networks with natives of the host culture. Stan, Mark, and Tom developed connections into a second order zone social network, allowing for more practice in functions of more advanced oral ability. What was also shown is that the motivational orientation (integrative, instrumental, or intrinsic) of four of the learners changed to another type during the stay abroad depending on the ability of the learner to interact in social networks. For example, Mark began the program with an intrinsic motivational orientation, which involves the arousal and maintenance of curiosity and can fluctuate as a result of such factors as learners' particular interests. By the end of the program, however, his motivational orientation had changed to an integrative one, where he may chose to learn the L2 because he was interested in the people and culture represented by the target-language group. The fact that he had developed a very strong social network and had very positive experiences with the members in that network helped him maintain this new motivation. He became so interested in the culture that he decided to extend his stay abroad.

Stan, who was integratively motivated at the start of the program, had no trouble maintaining his motivation due to his success in interacting in a social network, with no fluctuation in motivational orientation. Jennifer, Mark, and Tom, who began the program with an instrumental motivation, which associates a desire of learning the second language with a recognition of more practical merits of learning the target language, all experienced different fluctuations in their motivational orientation. Jennifer, who had failed to create a social network and reported negative experiences, had no motivation by the end of the program. Mark and Tom, who had success in creating a social network, changed from an instrumental motivation to an integrative and intrinsic motivational orientation throughout the rest of the stay abroad. On the other hand, Mark, who began with intrinsic motivation at the beginning of the program, fostered an integrative motivation by the end of the semester. The fact that he had developed a very strong social network and had very positive experiences with the members in that network helped him maintain this new motivation. He became so interested in the culture that he decided to extend his stay abroad.

Segalowitz & Freed (2004) indicate that initial oral ability levels may influence learners' predispositions to make use of extracurricular communicative opportunities, but the data here show that the learners' continued motivation to learn the target language was not directly influenced by their second language achievement or vice versa. Instead, their motivation was influenced by their success in incorporating themselves into social networks. As stated earlier, the interaction with native speakers that took place in the social networks fostered opportunities for negotiation, attention to gaps in feedback, and restructuring in the interlanguage. In other words, there is a conduit between motivation and language acquisition in the study abroad context, which is interaction within social networks with native target-language speakers.

The learners in this study went abroad with the intention of gaining a rewarding experience. Once there, all the learners invariably went through all or some of Bennett's (1986) six stages of acculturation. At the beginning of the program, the learners were in one of the three beginning stages; that is, they maintained ethnocentrism. All learners showed various degrees of preserving hegemony of their American culture over the Argentine. Throughout the program, however, all but Jennifer showed progression, some more than others, into the state of ethnorelativism (or acculturation) in which the learners acknowledged the possibility of differences amongst the two cultures.

The difference in learner progress through these states of cultural awareness is linked to their experiences, motivation, personalities, and abilities to handle difficult new situations. The learners who remained at the state in which they preserved the hegemony of their culture over the new host culture maintained a negative attitude toward the host culture. This attitude invariably influenced with whom they chose to interact, most likely an American. Because they spent much time with fellow Americans and interacted regularly in English instead of Spanish, there was a lack of development in their linguistic accuracy and oral communication skills in Spanish.

Being in the study abroad environment for an extended period of time allowed the learners opportunities to create, foster, and maintain motivation and social networks with the target culture. This experience allowed the learners to recognize, minimize, and finally accept cultural differences, which resulted in an impetus for learning, providing the learners the chance to work their way to understanding and to interaction.

What is the minimal amount of time students should spend abroad to benefit linguistically from the experience?

This question is difficult since it is open to different perspectives. In terms of this study, linguistic benefit is seen in positive development in second language linguistic accuracy and oral communication skills. In order to benefit linguistically, the learner must have ample time to go through the normal stages of cultural awareness. Although these stages may vary for learners, some remain in a rut of isolation from the host culture. In those cases, the learner usually gives up hope of assimilating and understanding the culture and, in turn, gives up on integrating into target language social networks in which language development occurs. The learner that perseveres through the sometimes-difficult first stage finds that the situation eventually improves, even in the worst cases. What was found in this study was that, by the fourth month, the learner usually established a social network in the host culture, some more extensive than others. Likewise, an overall development and stability was seen in linguistic development, although more time was needed to develop more advanced oral communication skills.

It is recommended that a learner spend a minimum of four months in a study abroad program to benefit linguistically. The learner must keep in mind the interdependency of interaction in the environment and language acquisition. Only then will the learner be motivated to maintain social networks in which opportunities arise to practice advanced oral communication skills. In the end, the study abroad students must understand the effect that perseverance has over their language acquisition process. Language acquisition in the study abroad context is a non-linear process that necessitates active participation in order to show development. The study abroad context offers many opportunities to practice these skills but it is ultimately the learner's decision to make the experience a fruitful one.

Conclusions

As mentioned in the Introduction, without research that focuses on the inter-dependence of interaction in the host environment and language acquisition, learners will not understand the effect that perseverance has over their language acquisition process. The findings of the present project show that study abroad offers opportunities to build social networks and interact with native speakers and those that take advantage of this opportunity and seek to use the target language are the ones who make the most progress, providing evidence for Freed's (1995a) assumption in this matter.

While there were learners who tried to incorporate themselves into new social networks, there were others who did not. The learners in this study that showed an "investment" in learning the L2 and had high motivation were those that had more extended networks (2nd order zones), which correlated with gains in linguistic accuracy. Although Churchill (in press) and Wilkinson (1998) have found that missed opportunities for interaction and less development in language could be due to the fact that some institutional and environmental factors may increase distance between students and the host culture, other research, including the present, has shown additional possibilities. The data from this study shows that the unwillingness to interact and create social networks with the speakers of the host culture stemmed from motivational and attitudinal deficits maintained by the learner, as has been shown in previous research (Citron, 1995; Gardner, 1985; Gardner & Lambert, 1959). Hassall (in press) makes similar conclusions that motivation is the key to understanding learners' behavior abroad and those who reject opportunities for interaction lack a sufficiently strong motivation to learn the language. Segalowitz & Freed (2004) add another reason as to why some learners did not incorporate themselves into networks, in that some learners are just different in "how ready they are linguistically and cognitively to seize the opportunities provided and to benefit from them once they do" (p. 196).

The learners in this study that had high motivation were those that had more extended networks, which correlated with gains in linguistic accuracy and development in oral ability functions and fluency. On the other hand, those with low motivation had weak social networks that correlated with no development in functions. Milroy (1980) instructed field workers that the way to collect reliable conversational data was through their incorporation into second order zone social networks. Incorporation into social networks also proved to be valuable for the learners in this study for development of linguistic and oral communication skills since the multiplex relationships that were developed in the networks aided the learner in being part of more extended conversations. Interacting within these social situations allowed the learner to practice certain second language linguistic aspects and oral communication skills in a more thorough manner, speaking on topics and in functions beyond everyday speech. An English-speaking learner that is with other English speakers rarely addresses conversational topics in the second language.

Within an second language multiplex network in which all acquaintances deal with each other in more than one capacity, the native speaker friends want elaboration of certain experiences or opinions, drawing the learner into the network's mesh of exchange and obligation relationships and increasing the learner's participation in interactions with native speakers. Although I am not making a conclusion on the necessary length or content that these interactions must have, I do assume that a study abroad student needs to learn strategies to build new social networks and share opinions within that group of acquaintances since it is an important aspect of maintaining a network. These interactions within extended or meaningful social networks provide little opportunity to avoid certain topics that are difficult to express. Participating in interactions with native speakers pushes oral communication skills to develop. Research by Cohen (1998) of strategies in learning and using a second language refers to language learning strategies as "processes which are consciously selected by learners and which may result in action taken to enhance the learning of the use of the second foreign language" (p. 4). That is, the learner needs to make a conscious decision to make social networks and interact within them. Cohen (2000) adds that "social strategies" (Chamot 1987; Oxford 1990) include "the actions learners chose to take as so to interact with other learners and with proficient second-language speakers (e.g., asking questions to clarify social roles and relationships and cooperating with others to complete tasks)" (p.3).

At the same time, the input that the learners are exposed to in such interactions at first is often beyond their comprehension, leading them to negotiate for meaning by asking clarification questions. Through this interaction the learners may also notice gaps in their production by comparing it to what their native counterpart is saying, as was similarly noted by Gass and Varonis (1994). Not only do the learners notice gaps and improve linguistic accuracy but they also may apply more advanced communicative skills to their developing interlanguage through scaffolding strategies, as noted by Lantolf and Appel (1994) and Donato (1994). Collentine (2004) even offers an explanation as to why there is a perception in research that the study abroad environment has a positive effect on learners, "It may be that day-to-day interactions with the target culture permit SA [study abroad] learners to practice retelling their daily or weekend adventures to friends and host-family members, and so they learn to produce numerous narrative behaviors within a given turn, which would also entail improvements in their abilities to generate a series of episodes" (p. 245). Segalowitz and Freed (2004, p. 174) also conclude that the study abroad learners "may not always avail themselves of the opportunities to be found in SA [study abroad] contexts" reasoning that the "students may be overwhelmed by the amount, delivery rate and complexity of the language that surrounds them, especially when their NS interlocutors do not accommodate by adjusting their speech to the students' linguistic limitations (as in 'foreigner talk')".

From the data in this study I have also learned that learners are sometimes rebuffed by a new group of acquaintances. Some learners give up while others persevere, trying and trying again, learning strategies to align themselves with people of a different culture in order to be more easily accepted into a social network of friends. The data in this study show that the learners who incorporate themselves into social networks are the ones who align themselves to the new culture through volunteering at a local church, traveling long distances to visit with friends of friends, and becoming tolerant of cultural annoyances.

The conclusions of this study, therefore, present more data among the contradictory evidence that informal, out-of-class contact may or may not enhance acquisition (Freed, 1995a). In this study, the learners that were self-motivated to maintain social networks and that practiced linguistic and oral communication skills not otherwise allowed to them, are evidence that informal, out-of-class contact can greatly enhance acquisition, if they choose to take advantage of this opportunity. It also shows the same theme that Atkinson (2002) emphasizes in his conclusions, "thought, feeling, and activity in the social world are brought together in the form of human beings actively operating as part of that world" (p. 539).

It is important to inform numerous study abroad organizations about unrealistic goals that they may promise to the learners to recruit them. It is also important to inform the programs of the other elements that need to be fostered during a stay abroad. For one, the need for ways to successfully create social networks, such as: including a required volunteer program while abroad, as suggested by Twombly (1995); incorporating as part of the curriculum internships with local businesses or universities; or, by including independent projects that require the L2 learner to interview various native speakers on distinct topics through out their stay abroad.

According to the data that have yet to be tested on a larger population of learners, high motivation and positive attitudes do not correlate to development in linguistic accuracy but they do correlate to development of oral ability functions. It is quite evident that attitudes, motivation, and environment play a significant role in the second language acquisition process. Such research instruments as social network logs and personal diaries provide a window into the actions and feelings of those study abroad participants in the process of acquiring the target language. It is important to observe successful learners who take advantage of participating in native social networks and what the impact of a lack of such participation is on their language acquisition process. By uncovering this information, learners can be instructed before going abroad of the importance of perseverance in creating and maintaining social networks of the people of the host culture.

Moreover, learners can be forewarned about the stages of acculturation they may experience before arriving at a point where they will want to be part of the host culture. Typical study abroad programs do include orientation periods at the beginning of the stay abroad in which the student has time (usually two weeks) to reduce the initial overwhelming feelings of being in a foreign country. This study found that learners usually took few months to overcome those feelings. There are many examples of what learners tend to do to alleviate feelings of culture shock. Advice should be given that culture shock is temporary and the solution should not be to turn to fellow students who speak the same language and are in the same situation. Having information on hand that shows what staying within the "dense" population of fellow English-speaking study abroad learners does to the second language acquisition process, which in turn should motivate learners to establish and broaden their social networks to include native speakers with whom to have significant interaction.

Directions for Future Research

This case study of the acquisition processes in the naturalistic setting provides relevant information for the study abroad student as to what to expect during the program and how to take most advantage of the time spent abroad. A future research direction would be to focus on the similarities and differences that exist in the acquisition processes of classroom and naturalistic settings, including the domestic immersion program and study abroad program (see *Studies in Second Language Acquisition,* volume 26).

An obvious direction is where this study falls short, in actually audio taping learners in many of their interactions in the networks to see if they actually do practice advanced level speech functions, notice gaps, restructure their output, and show motivation with native speakers. Also, following one of Segalowitz and Freed's (2004) suggestions to find out why a learning environment proves beneficial for some learners and not others, "it may be more fruitful to inquire into the dynamics of learner-context interactions" (p. 3).

Another interesting direction would be to add to the scarce pool of research carried out on the advantages of study abroad programs in which non-classroom activities are emphasized. According to Freed (1993), the most interesting finding from such research was that learners who were in work placements abroad, as opposed to university programs, tended to demonstrate "superiority on a number of measures." As an extension from that research environment, data can be collected to investigate alignment strategies, looking at ways in which learners work ways to align themselves linguistically with people of second language cultures. Some current alignment literature deals with such interactional discourse systems among speakers as turn taking, physical orientations, and contextualization cues that may be culturally defined. Gumperz (1982) points out that individuals who share identical linguistic systems may have markedly different interactional systems, causing misunderstandings and prejudices. Future research may focus on how study abroad learners avoid misunderstanding and prejudices and linguistically align themselves with other speakers in order to create an integrative network.

Appendix A
BACKGROUND QUESTIONNAIRES

<u>Foreign language and culture background questionnaire</u>
1. Have you lived outside the US?   Yes   No
2. Have you wanted to live outside the US?   Yes   No
3. Have you traveled outside the US?   Yes   No
4. Do you use a language besides English/Spanish?   Yes   No
5. Does your family use a language besides English?   Yes   No
6. Have you studied languages besides Spanish?   Yes   No

<u>Student background information questionnaire</u>
1. Male   Female
2. Freshman   Sophomore   Junior   Senior   Graduate
3. Years of Spanish taken:
4. Reasons for learning Spanish:
_____
_____

5. Expectations of study abroad program outcome:
_____
_____

6. What plans do you have after your study abroad experience as far as learning Spanish?
_____
_____

Appendix B
INTERVIEW MATERIALS

Each interview will contain the following questions: (a) greeting; (b) leading questions; and (c) prompts to elicit details depending on the learners' story.

<u>Possible Greetings</u>

How are you?

Is everything going all right?

<u>Possible Lead Questions</u>

What was one of the best moments you've had so far?

Did a memorable or funny incident happen?

Tell me about your trip to _____?

Did you have any interesting or difficult experiences?

Do you remember the first day you arrived to Buenos Aires?

How did you choose to study abroad in Argentina?

What did you have to do in preparation to come to Argentina?

What has impressed you most about Buenos Aires? Is there something you like/dislike?

Tell me about your host family.

<u>Possible Prompts to Elicit Responses</u>

And what happened?

Describe _____?

It always interests me how people meet. How did you meet _____?

What else have you seen in Argentina/South America? Why?

Appendix C
NETWORK CONTACT LOGS (Vann, 1996)

Instructions

Please fill out the following forms for seven consecutive days using a new form for each day. Indicate what activity you are involved in by placing the name of the person with whom you carry out the activity, and in which language (S=Spanish, E= English) in which the interaction occurs. If you carry out the activity with a group, put "&" between the names, and/or if you carry out the same activity with two people at two different times, put a slash "/" between the names.

Example

You eat breakfast and dinner with your host mother and father and you speak with each other in Spanish. The same day you go with your friend Sam to have some coffee, and you speak with each other in English. Later on you have some coffee with your friend Victor, and you speak with each other in Spanish.

This should be represented in the following manner

Date:	Name(s)
Today I had breakfast with	host mother (S) & host father (S)
Today I had lunch with	
Today I had dinner with	host mother (S) & host father (S)
Today I had coffee with	Sam (E) / Victor (S)

Date:	Name(s)
Today I had breakfast with	
Today I had lunch with	
Today I had dinner with	
Today I had coffee with	
Today I phoned	
Today I received a phone call from	
Today I went out with	
Today I studied with	
Today I talked at least 10 minutes with	
Today I argued with	
Today I persuaded/convinced	
Today I told a story to	
Today I smoked with	
Today I went out for a drink with	
Other activities: Today I _____ with	

BIBLIOGRAPHY

American Council on the Teaching of Foreign Languages. (1986). *ACTFL proficiency guidelines*. New York: Hastings on Hudson.

Andersen, R. W. (1990). Models, processes, principles, and strategies: Second language acquisition in and out of the classroom. In B. VanPatten & J. Lee (Eds.), *Second language acquisition: Foreign language learning* (pp. 45-78). Clevedon, UK: Multilingual Matters.

Atkinson, D. (2002) Toward a sociocognitive approach to second language acquisition. *The Modern Language Journal* 86 (4), 525-545.

Bacon, S. (1995). Coming to grips with the culture: Another use of dialogue journals in teacher education. *Foreign Language Annals, 28*, 193-207.

Beebe, L. (1980). Measuring the use of communication strategies. In R. Scarsella & S. Krashen (Eds.), *Research in second language acquisition* (pp. 39-66). Rowely, MA: Newbury House.

Bennett, M. J. (1986). Towards ethnorelativism: A developmental model of intercultural sensitivity. In R. M. Paige (Ed.), *Cross-cultural orientation: New conceptualizations and applications* (pp. 27-69). New York: University Press of America.

Block, D. (1996). Not so fast: Some thoughts on theory culling, relativism, accepted findings and the heart and soul of SLA. *Applied Linguistics, 17*, 63-83.

Blom, P., & Gumperz, J. (1972). Social meaning in linguistic structures: Code switching in Norway. In J. Gumperz & D. Hymes (Eds.), *Directions in sociolinguistics* (pp. 407-434). New York: Rinehart and Winston.

Brecht, R., Davidson, D., & Ginsberg, R. (1993). Predictors of foreign language gain during study abroad. *NFLC Occasional Papers*. Washington, DC: National Foreign Language Center.

Brecht, R., & Robinson, J. L. (1993). Qualitative analysis of second language acquisition in study abroad: The ACTR/NFLC project. *NFLC Occasional Papers*. Washington, DC: National Foreign Language Center.

Breiner-Sanders, K., Lowe, P., Miles, J., & Swender, E. (2000). ACTFL Proficiency Guidelines-Speaking Revised 1999. *Foreign Language Annals, 33.1,* 13-18.

Brown, H. D. (1995). *Principles of language learning and teaching.* New Jersey: Prentice Hall Regents.

Byrnes H., & Canale, M. (Eds.). (1987). *Defining and developing proficiency: Guidelines, implementations, and concepts.* Chicago: National Textbook Company.

Carroll, J. (1967). Foreign language proficiency levels attained by language majors near graduation from college. *Foreign Language Annals, 1,* 131-151.

Chamot, A. U. (1987). The learning strategies of ESL students. In A. Wenden & J. Rubin (Eds.), *Learner strategies in language learning.* Englewood Cliffs, NJ: Prentice-Hall.

Churchill, E. (in press). Variability in the study abroad classroom and learner competence. In M. DuFon & E. Churchill (Eds.), *Language learners in study abroad contexts.*

Citron, J. L. (1995). Can cross-cultural understanding aid second language acquisition? Toward a theory of ethno-lingual relativity. *Hispania, 78,* 105-113.

Clark, J. L. D., & Li, Y. (1986). *Development, validation, and dissemination of a proficiency based test of speaking ability in Chinese and an associated assessment model for other less commonly taught languages.* Washington, DC: Center for Applied Linguistics. ERIC Document Reproduction Service No. ED 278 264.

Cohen, A. D. (1998). *Strategies in learning and using a second language.* Essex, UK: Longman.

Cohen, A. D. (2000). Strategies-based instruction for learners of a second language. *NASSP Bulletin, 84,* 10-18.

Collentine, J. (2004). The effects of learning contexts on morphosyntactic and lexical development. *Studies in Second Language Acquisition, 26,* 227-248.

Cubitt, T. (1973). Network density among urban families. In J. Boissevain & J. C. Mitchell (Eds.), *Network analysis: Studies in human interaction* (pp. 67-82). The Hague: Mouton.

Day, J. T. (1987). Student motivation, academic validity, and the summer language program abroad: An editorial. *Modern Language Journal, 71*, 261-266.

DeKeyser, R. M. (1986). From learning to acquisition? Foreign language development in a US classroom and during a semester abroad. Unpublished doctoral dissertation, Stanford University.

DeKeyser, R. M. (1991). Foreign language development during a semester abroad. In B. Freed (Ed.), *Foreign language acquisition research and the classroom* (pp. 104-119). Lexington, MA: DC Heath.

De Ley, H. (1975). Organized programs of study in France: Some contributions of stranger theory. *The French Review, 48*, 836-847.

Dewey, D. (2004). A comparison of reading development by learners of Japanese in intensive domestic immersion and study abroad contexts. *Studies in Second Language Acqusition, 26* (2), 303-328.

Díaz-Campos, M. (2004). Context of learning in the acquisition of Spanish second language phonology. *Studies in Second Language Acquisition, 26,* 249-273.

Donato, R. (1994). Collective scaffolding in second language learning. In J. P. Lantolf & G. Appel (Eds.), *Vygotskian approaches to second language research* (pp. 33-56). Norwood, NJ: Ablex.

Dörnyei, Z., & Scott, M. L. (1997). Communication strategies in a second language: Definitions and taxonomies. *Language Learning, 47(1),* 173-210.

Doughty, D. (1979). *Word meaning and Montague grammar: The semantics of verbs and times in generative semantics and in Montague's PTQ.* Boston: D. Reidel.

Dowell, M-M. (1995). Changing perspectives toward the target culture among selected participants in a study abroad program in Cuernavaca, Morelos, Mexico. In *Research perspectives in adult language learning and acquisition-study abroad: Research on learning language and culture in context* (pp. 1-8). Columbus, OH: National Foreign Language Resource Center.

Ellis, R. (1998). *Second language acquisition.* Oxford: Oxford University Press.

Ejzenberg, R. (1992). Understanding nonnative oral fluency: The role of task structure and discourse variability. Unpublished educational doctoral dissertation, State University of New York, Albany.

Ferguson, C. (1995). Foreword. In B. Freed (Ed.), *Second language acquisition in a study abroad context* (pp. xi- xv). Amsterdam: John Benjamins.

Firth, A., & Wagner, J. (1997). On discourse, communication, and (some) fundamental concepts in SLA research. *Modern Language Journal, 81,* 285-300.

Frank, V. (1997, March) *Potential negative effects of homestay.* Paper presented at the meeting of the Middle Atlantic Conference of the American Association for the Advancement of Slavic Studies, Albany, NY.

Freed, B. (1990a). Current realities and future prospects in foreign language acquisition research. In B. Freed (Ed.), *Foreign language acquisition research and the classroom* (pp. 3-27). Lexington, MA: DC Heath.

Freed, B. (1990b). Language learning in a study abroad context: The effects of interactive and non-interactive out-of-class contact on grammatical achievement and oral proficiency. In J. Atlantis (Ed.), *Linguistics, language teaching and language acquisition: The interdependence of theory, practice and research (GURT 1990)* (pp. 459-477). Washington, DC: Georgetown University Press.

Freed, B. (1993). Assessing the linguistic impact of study abroad: What we currently know--what we need to know. *Journal of Asian Pacific Communication, 4,* 151-166.

Freed, B. (1995a). Language learning and study abroad. In B. Freed (Ed.), *Second language acquisition in a study abroad context* (pp. 3-34). Philadelphia: John Benjamins.

Freed, B. (1995b). What makes us think that students who study abroad become fluent? In B. Freed (Ed.), *Second language acquisition in a study abroad context* (pp. 123-148). Philadelphia: John Benjamins.

Freed, B. (1998). An overview of issues and research in language learning in a study abroad setting. *Frontiers: The Interdisciplinary Journal of Study Abroad, 4,* 31-60.

Freed, B. F., Dewey, D. P., & Segalowitz. (2004). The Language Contact Profile. *Studies in Second Language Acquisition, 26,* 349-356.

Freed, B., Segalowitz, N., & Dewey, D. (2004). Context of learning and second language fluency in French: Comparing regular classroom, study abroad and intensive domestic immersion programs. *Studies in Second Language Acquisition, 26,* 275-301.

Freed, B., So, S., & Lazar, N. (2003). Language learning abroad: How do gains in written fluency compare with gains in oral fluency in French as a second language? *ADFL Bulletin, 34(3),* 34-40.

Gal, S. (1979). *Language shift: Social determinants of linguistic change in bilingual Austria.* New York: Academic Press.

Galloway, V. (1987). From defining to developing proficiency: A look at the decisions. In H. Byrnes & M. Canale (Eds.), *Defining and developing proficiency: Guidelines, implementations, and concepts. In conjunction with the American Council on the Teaching of Foreign Languages* (pp. 25-74). Lincolnwood, IL: National Textbook Company.

Gardner, R. C. (1985). *Social psychology and second language learning: The role of attitudes and motivations.* London: Edward Arnold.

Gardner, R. C., & Lambert, W. E. (1959). Motivational variables in second language acquisition. *Canadian Journal of Psychology, 13,* 266-272.

Gardner, R. C., & Lambert, W. E. (1972). *Attitudes and motivation in second language learning.* Rowley, MA: Newbury House.

Gardner, R. C., & MacIntyre, P. D. (1991). An instrumental motivation in language study: Who says it isn't effective? *Studies in Second Language Learning, 13,* 57-72.

Gardner, R. C., & Smythe, P. C. (1975). Motivation and second language acquisition. *The Canadian Modern Language Review, 31,* 218-230.

Gass, S. (1997). *Input, interaction, and the second language learner.* Mahwah, NJ: Lawrence Erlbaum Associates.

Gass, S., & Varonis, E. (1994). Input, interaction, and second language production. *Studies in Second Language Acquisition, 16,* 283-302.

Gass, S., & Selinker, L. (1994). *Second language acquisition: An introductory course*. New Jersey: Lawrence Erlbaum Associates.

Gumperz, J. J. (1982). *Discourse strategies*. Cambridge, UK: Cambridge University Press.

Hassall, T. (in press). Learning to take leave in social conversations: A diary study. In M. DuFon & E. Churchill (Eds.), *Language learners in study abroad contexts*.

Heller, M. (1987). The role of language in the formation of ethnic identity. In J. Phinney and M. Rotheram (Eds.), *Children's ethnic socialization* (pp. 180-200). Newbury Park, CA: Sage.

Higgs, T., & Clifford, R. (1982). The push toward communication. In T. Higgs (Ed.), *Curriculum, competence and the foreign language teacher* (pp. 57-59). Skokie, IL: National Textbook Company.

Howard, M. (2001). The effects of study abroad on the L2 learner's structural skills: Evidence from advanced learners of French. *EUROSLA Yearbook, 1*, 123-141.

Huebner, T. (1995). The effects of overseas language programs. In B. Freed (Ed.), *Second language acquisition in a study abroad context* (pp. 171-193). Philadelphia: John Benjamins.

Isabelli, C. A. (2003). Study abroad for advanced foreign language majors: Optimal duration for developing complex structures. In H. Byrnes & H. Maxim (Eds.), *Advanced foreign language learner: A challenge to college programs (AAUSC series)* (pp. 114-130). Boston: Heinle.

Isabelli, C. A. (2004). The acquisition of Null Subject Parameter properties in SLA: Some effects of positive evidence in a natural learning context. *Hispania, 87.1*, 150-162.

Kaplan, M. A. (1989). French in the community: A survey of language used abroad. *The French Review, 63*, 290-299

Kellerman, E. (1985). If at first you do succeed... In S. Gass & C. Madden (Eds.), *Input in second language acquisition*. Rowley, MA: Newbury.

Krashen, S. (1985). *The input hypothesis: Issues and implications*. London: Longman.

Krashen, S., & Seliger, H. (1976). The role of formal and informal environments in second language learning: A pilot study. *International Journal of Psycholinguistics, 3*, 15-20.

Krashen, S., Seliger, H., & Harnett, D. (1974). Two studies in adult second language learning. *Kritikon Literarum, 2*, 220-8.

Krzic, G. (1995). A study of Japanese and American intercultural relations and learning. In Research perspectives in adult language learning and acquisition-study abroad: Research on learning language and culture in context (pp. 85-108). Columbus, OH: National Foreign Language Resource Center.

Lafford, B. (1995). Getting into, through and out of a survival situation: A comparison of communicative strategies used by students studying Spanish abroad and 'at home.' In B. Freed (Ed.), Second Language Acquisition in a Study Abroad Context (pp. 97-121). Philadelphia: John Benjamins.

Lafford, B. (2004). The effect of the context of learning on the use of communication strategies by learners of Spanish as a second language. *Studies in Second Language Acquisition, 26*, 201-225.

Lafford, B., & Collentine, J. (1989). The telltale targets: An analysis of access errors in the speech of intermediate students of Spanish. *Lenguas Modernas, 16*, 143-162.

Lafford, B. A., & Ryan, J. (1996). The acquisition of lexical meaning in a study abroad context: The Spanish prepositions por and para. *Hispania, 78*, 528-547.

Lantolf, J. P., & Appel, G. (1994). Theoretical framework: An introduction to Vygotskian perspectives on second language research. In J. P. Lantolf & G. Appel (Eds.), *Vygotskian approaches to second language research* (pp. 1-32). Norwood, NJ: Ablex.

Lapkin, S., Hart, D., & Swain, M. (1995). A Canadian interprovincial exchange: Evaluating the linguistic impact of a three-month stay in Quebec. In B. Freed (Ed.), *Second language acquisition in a study abroad context* (pp. 67-94). Philadelphia: John Benjamins.

Lazar, N. (2004). A short survey on causal inference, with implications for context of learning studies of second language acquisition. *SSLA, 26* (2), 329-347.

Lennon, P. (1990a). Investigating fluency in EFL: A quantitative approach. *Language Learning, 40*, 387-417.

Lennon, P. (1990b). The advanced learner at large in the L2 community: Developments in spoken performance. *IRAL, 28*, 309-324.

Lightbown, P. (1985). Great expectations: Second language acquisition research and classroom teaching. *Applied Linguistics, 6*, 173-189.

Liskin-Gasparro, J. (1993). *Talking about the past: An analysis of the discourse in intermediate high and advanced level speakers of Spanish.* Unpublished doctoral dissertation, University of Texas, Austin.

Liskin-Gasparro, J. (1996). Circumlocution, communication strategies, and the ACTFL proficiency guidelines: An analysis of student discourse. *Foreign Language Annals, 29*, 317-330.

Liskin-Gasparro, J., & Urdaneta, L. (1995). Language learning in a semester abroad: The spring 1995 University of Iowa Universidad de los Andes program in Merida, Venezuela. In *Research perspectives in adult language learning and acquisition-study abroad: Research on learning language and culture in context* (pp. 138-160). Columbus, OH: National Foreign Language Resource Center.

Long, M. (1981). Input, interaction, and second language acquisition. In H. Winitz (Ed.), *Native language and foreign language acquisition* (pp. 259-278). Annals of the New York Academy of Sciences, 379.

Marriot, H. (1995). The acquisition of politeness patterns by exchange students in Japan. In B. Freed (Ed.), *Second language acquisition in a study abroad context* (pp. 197-224). Philadelphia: John Benjamins.

Milleret, M. (1990). Evaluation and the summer language program abroad: A review essay. *Modern Language Journal, 74*, 483-488.

Milleret, M. (1991). Assessing the gain in oral proficiency from summer foreign study. *ADFL, 22*, 39-43.

Milroy, L. (1980). *Language and social networks.* Baltimore: University Park Press.

Milroy, L. (1987). *Observing and analyzing natural language: A critical account of sociolinguistic method.* Oxford: Blackwell Press.

Moehle, D. (1984). A comparison of the second language speech of different native speakers. In H. Dechert, D. Moehle, & M. Raupach. (Eds.), *Second language production* (pp. 26-49). Tübingen, Germany: Gunter Narr.

Naiman, N., Fröhlich, M., Stern, H., & Todesco, A. (1978). *The good language learner: Research in education series no. 7*. Toronto: Ontario Institute for Studies in Education.

Olynyk, M., d'Angeljan, A., & Sankoff, D. (1990). A quantitative and qualitative analysis of speech markers in the native and second language speech of bilinguals. In R. Scarcella, R. Andersen, & S. Krashen (Eds.), *Developing communicative competence in a second language* (pp. 139-155). Rowley, MA: Newbury House.

Oxford, R. (1990). *Language learning strategies: What every teacher should know*. New York: Newbury House/HarperCollins.

Oxford, R., & Crookall, D. (1989). Research on language learning strategies: Methods, findings, and instructional issues. *Modern Language Journal, 73*, 404-419.

Peirce, B. N. (1995). Social identity, investment, and language learning. *TESOL Quarterly, 29(1)*, 9-31.

Pellegrino, V. A. (1998). Student perspectives on language learning in a study abroad context. *Frontiers: The Interdisciplinary Journal of Study Abroad, 4*, 91-120.

Pica, T. (1987). Second language acquisition, social interaction, and the classroom. *Applied Linguistics, 8*, 3-21.

Polanyi, L. (1982). Linguistic and social constraints on storytelling. *Journal of Pragmatics, 6*, 509-824.

Polanyi, L. (1989). *Telling the American story: A structural and cultural analysis of conversational storytelling*. Cambridge: MIT Press.

Polanyi, L. (1995). Language learning and living abroad: Stories from the field. In B. Freed (Ed.), *Second language acquisition in a study abroad context* (pp. 271-292). Philadelphia: John Benjamins.

Raupach, M. (1983). Analysis and evaluation of communicative strategies. In C. Færch, & G. Kasper (Eds.), *Strategies in interlanguage communication* (pp. 199-201). London: Longman.

Raupach, M. (1984). Formulae in second language speech production. In H. Dechert (Ed.), *Second language productions* (pp. 114-137). Tübingen, Germany: Gunter Narr.

Regan, V. (1995). The acquisition of sociolinguistic native speech norms. In B. Freed (Ed.), *Second language acquisition in a study abroad context* (pp. 245-267). Philadelphia: John Benjamins.

Regan, V. (1998). Sociolinguistics and language learning in a study abroad context. In B. Freed (Ed.), *Language learning in a study abroad context* (pp. 61-120). Special issue of *Frontiers: The Interdisciplinary Journal of Study Abroad.*

Rubin, J. (1975). What the 'good language learner' can teach us. *TESOL Quarterly, 9,* 41-51.

Ryan, J., & Lafford, B. A. (1992). Acquisition of lexical meaning in a study abroad environment: Ser and estar and the Granada experience. *Hispania, 75,* 714-722.

Schumann, J. H. (1976). Social distance as a factor in second language acquisition. *Language Learning, 26,* 135-143.

Schumann, J. H. (1978). *The pidginization process: A model for second language acquisition.* Rowley, MA: Newbury House.

Segalowitz, N., & Freed, B. (2004). Context, contact and cognition in oral fluency acquisition: Learning Spanish in "at home" and "study abroad" contexts. *Studies in Second Language Acquisition, 26,* 173-199.

Shohamy, E., Gordon, C., Kenyon, D. M., & Stansfield, C. W. (1989). The development and validation of a semi direct test for assessing oral proficiency in Hebrew. *Bulletin of Hebrew Higher Education, 4,* 4-9.

Siegal, M. (1995). Individual differences and study abroad: Women learning Japanese in Japan. In B. Freed (Ed.), *Second language acquisition in a study abroad context* (pp. 225-244). Philadelphia: John Benjamins.

Smith, C. (1991). *The parameter of aspect.* Boston: Kluwer Academic Publishers.

Spada, N. (1985). Effects of informal contact on classroom learners' proficiency: A review of five studies. *TESL Canada Journal, 2,* 51-62.

Spada, N. (1986). The interaction between type of contact and type of instruction: Some effects on the second language proficiency of adult learners. *Studies in Second Language Acquisition, 8*, 181-199.

Spanish Teachers Chatboard. (2000, January 2). Texas oral proficiency test. Message posted to http://www.teachers.net/mentors/spanish/topic83/1.02.00.17.12.43.htm

Spradley, J. (1979). *The ethnographic interview.* New York: Harcourt Brace Jovanovich.

Stansfield, C. W. (1990). An evaluation of simulated oral proficiency interviews as measures of spoken language proficiency. In J. Atlantis (Ed.), *Georgetown University round table on language and linguistics* (pp. 228-234). Washington, DC: Georgetown University Press.

Stansfield, C. W., & Kenyon, D. M. (1996). Simulated oral proficiency interview: An update. Retrieved May 23, 2000, from ERIC Languages and Linguistics Digest - Center for Applied Linguistics database http://www.cal.org/ericcll/digest/stansf02.html

Stansfield, C. W., Kenyon, D. M., Paiva, R., Doyle, F., Ulsh, I., & Cowles, M. A. (1990). The development and validation of the Portuguese speaking test. *Hispania, 73*, 641-651.

Temple, L. (1992). Disfluencies in learner speech. *Australian Review of Applied Linguistics, 15*, 29-44.

Terrell, T. D., & Salgués de Cargill, M. (1979). *Lingüística aplicada a la enseñanza del español a anglohablantes.* New York: John Wiley and Sons.

Towell, R., Hawkins, R., & Bazergui, N. (1996). The development of fluency in advanced learners of French. *Applied Linguistics, 17*, 84-119.

Twombly, S. B. (1995) Piropos and friendships: Gender and culture clash in study abroad. *Frontiers: The Interdisciplinary Journal of Study Abroad, 1* - Online document: http://www.frontiersjournal.com/back/one/ twom.htm

Vann, R. (1996). *Pragmatic and cultural aspects of an emergent language variety: The construction of Catalan Spanish deictic expressions.* Unpublished doctoral dissertation, University of Texas, Austin.

VanPatten, B. (1985). The acquisition of <u>ser</u> and <u>estar</u> by adult learners of Spanish: A preliminary investigation of transitional stages of competence. *Hispania, 68*, 399-406.

Véguez, R. (1984, April). *The oral proficiency interview and the junior year abroad: Some unexpected results.* Paper presented at the meeting of the Northeast Conference on the Teaching of Foreign Language, New York.

Vendler, Z. (1967). *Linguistics in philosophy.* Ithaca, NY: Cornell University Press.

Vygotsky, L. (1978). *Mind in society: The development of higher psychological processes.* Cambridge, MA: Harvard University Press.

Wilkinson, S. (1997, December). *Separating fact from myth: A qualitative perspective on language learning during summer study abroad.* Paper presented at the meeting of the Modern Language Association, Toronto.

Wilkinson, S. (1998). Study abroad from the participants' perspective: A challenge to common beliefs. *Foreign Language Annals, 31(1)*, 23-39.

AUTHOR INDEX

Andersen 67, 137
Appel 22, 141, 147
Atkinson 148
Bacon 17, 43
Bazergui 12, 56, 69, 133, 140
Beebe 91
Bennet 28, 43, 101, 102, 126, 131, 143
Block 6
Blom 23, 24
Brecht 2, 7, 15, 133
Brown 4, 63, 68
Byrnes 44, 88
Canale 44, 88
Carroll 2, 7, 133
Churchill 145
Citron 29, 30, 145
Cohen 146, 147
Collentine 3, 9, 10, 46, 133, 134, 138, 139, 147
Cubitt 58
Davidson 2, 7, 15, 133
Day 1
De Ley 110
DeKeyser 3, 8, 11, 16, 64, 133, 134
Dewey 9, 12, 17, 39, 55, 56, 133, 139
Díaz-Campos 3, 9, 133
Donato 22, 141, 147
Dörnyei 21, 56

Dowell 30, 43
Ellis 4, 62
Firth 18
Frank 17, 134
Freed 2-4, 6, 7, 9, 11, 12, 14, 16-18, 39, 40, 55, 56, 133, 134, 139, 142, 145, 147, 148, 150
Gal 58
Galloway 48
Gardner 4, 5, 30, 145
Gass 20-22, 104, 141, 147
Ginsberg 2, 7, 15, 133
Gumperz 23, 24, 150
Hart 8, 11, 18, 64, 134
Hassall 145
Hawkins 12, 56, 69, 133, 140
Heller 2
Howard 2, 9, 10, 133, 134
Huebner 8, 11, 36, 64, 134
Isabelli 2, 9, 10, 133, 136
Kaplan 2, 15, 133
Kellerman 68
Kenyon 40, 41
Krashen 16, 20, 134
Krzic 15
Lafford 3, 9-12, 18, 46, 55, 56, 133, 134, 139, 140
Lambert 4, 5, 30, 145
Lantolf 21, 22, 141, 147
Lapkin 8, 11, 18, 64, 134

Lazar 18
Lennon 2, 9, 10, 40, 55, 133, 134
Lightbown 21, 141
Liskin-Gasparro 2, 3, 51, 133
Long 20
MacIntyre 4, 5
Meara 133
Milleret 2, 15, 69, 133
Milroy 23-28, 96, 97, 138, 146
Milton 133
Moehle 3, 8, 11, 64, 134
Naiman 92
Peirce 2, 5, 98
Pellegrino 17, 134
Pica 20
Polanyi 2, 15, 48-51, 82, 133
Raupach 3, 8, 11, 64, 134
Robinson 7
Rubin 91

Ryan 9-11, 134
Schumann 14-16, 23, 28
Scott 21, 56
Segalowitz 3, 9, 12, 16, 17, 39, 55, 56, 133, 134, 139, 142, 145, 147, 150
Selinker 20
Smythe 4, 5
So 18
Spradley 31
Stansfield 40, 41
Swain 8, 11, 18, 64, 134
Towell 12, 56, 69, 133, 140
Twombly 148
Vann 58, 155
VanPatten 10
Varonis 20, 22, 105, 141, 148
Vygotsky 21, 22, 141
Wagner 18
Wilkinson 17, 134, 145

SUBJECT INDEX

ACTFL Guidelines 41, 48, 88

acculturation 18, 19, 28, 102, 113, 116, 126, 143, 149

attention 6, 20, 21, 22, 117, 137, 143

attitude 5, 18, 29, 30, 31, 32, 43, 57, 95, 96, 98, 102, 104, 106, 107, 113, 115, 117-119, 123-126, 128, 129, 131, 132, 134, 135, 141, 143, 149

backsliding 62-64, 66, 68, 69, 74, 77, 83, 84, 86, 89, 135, 136

comprehensible input 20, 22, 136, 137

confirmation checks 56

confirmation requests 56

diary 36, 42, 43, 57, 95, 96, 98, 99, 102, 106-109, 112, 114-117, 120-122, 125-127, 132

Distributional Bias Principal 67, 137

dysfluent 56

ethnocentrism 28, 101, 102, 126, 143

ethnolingual relativity 29, 30

ethnorelativism 28-30, 101, 102, 106, 131, 143

flow 3, 11, 27, 55, 56, 71, 78, 85, 88, 89, 90, 92, 93, 133, 139, 140

fluency 1, 4, 8, 11, 12, 38, 39, 55, 59, 85, 90-92, 105, 119, 133, 139, 146

gap 21, 22, 26, 32, 140, 141, 143, 147, 150

informal contact 134

Input Hypothesis 20

interaction 1, 2, 6, 7, 15, 17-27, 32, 58, 67, 97, 105, 112, 125, 129, 130, 134, 136, 138-141, 143-147, 149, 150, 155

investment 5, 98, 112, 119, 123, 131, 145

Monitor Model 20

motivation 2, 4-6, 14, 18, 23, 30-33, 37, 57, 58, 95, 96, 98, 104, 112, 113, 117, 119, 122, 124, 125, 129, 131, 132, 135, 138, 141-143, 145, 146, 149, 150

negotiation 20-22, 143

network contact log 42, 44, 96, 104, 108, 118, 124, 1129, 132

networks 1, 2, 16, 18, 22-28, 30-32, 43, 58, 95-98, 102-104, 113, 124, 131, 132, 135, 136, 140-140

noticing 21, 22, 24, 26, 128, 140, 147, 150

oral communication skills 11-14, 34, 48, 91

oral proficiency interview (OPI) 9, 11-13, 16, 36, 39, 40, 44, 48, 61, 62, 103, 111, 114, 123, 127

quantity of speech 3, 11, 39, 56, 71, 78, 85, 88, 90, 131, 133

restructuring 21, 26, 105, 143

SOPI 13, 36, 39, 40-42, 45, 55, 56, 59-62, 68, 70, 73, 98, 103, 106, 111, 114, 119, 123, 125, 127, 135

Texas Oral Proficiency Test 40

U-shaped behavior 62, 68

Zone of Proximal Development (ZPD) 2

MELLEN STUDIES IN EDUCATION

1. C. J. Schott, **Improving The Training and Evaluation of Teachers at the Secondary School Level: Educating the Educators in Pursuit of Excellence**
2. Manfred Prokop, **Learning Strategies For Second Language Users: An Analytical Appraisal with Case Studies**
3. Charles P. Nemeth, **A Status Report on Contemporary Criminal Justice Education: A Definition of the Discipline and an Assessment of Its Curricula, Faculty and Program Characteristics**
4. Stephen H. Barnes (ed.), **Points of View on American Higher Education: A Selection of Essays from** *The Chronicle of Higher Education* (Volume 1) **Professors and Scholarship**
5. Stephen H. Barnes (ed.), **Points of View on American Higher Education: A Selection of Essays from** *The Chronicle of Higher Education* (Volume 2) **Institutions and Issues**
6. Stephen H. Barnes (ed.), **Points of View on American Higher Education: A Selection of Essays from** *The Chronicle of Higher Education* (Volume 3) **Students and Standards**
7. Michael V. Belok and Thomas Metos, **The University President in Arizona 1945-1980: An Oral History**
8. Henry R. Weinstock and Charles J. Fazzaro, **Democratic Ideals and the Valuing of Knowledge In American Education: Two Contradictory Tendencies**
9. Arthur R. Crowell, Jr., **A Handbook For the Special Education Administrator: Organization and Procedures for Special Education**
10. J.J. Chambliss, **The Influence of Plato and Aristotle on John Dewey's Philosophy**
11. Alan H. Levy, **Elite Education and the Private School: Excellence and Arrogance at Phillips Exeter Academy**
12. James J. Van Patten (ed.), **Problems and Issues in College Teaching and Higher Education Leadership**
13. Célestin Freinet, **The Wisdom of Matthew: An Essay in Contemporary French Educational Theory**, John Sivell (trans.)
14. Francis R. Phillips, **Bishop Beck and English Education, 1949-1959**
15. Gerhard Falk, **The Life of the Academic Professional in America: An Inventory of Tasks, Tensions & Achievements**
16. Phillip Santa Maria, **The Question of Elementary Education in the Third Russian State Duma, 1907-1912**
17. James J. Van Patten (ed.), **The Socio-Cultural Foundations of Education and the Evolution of Education Policies in the U.S.**
18. Peter P. DeBoer, **Origins of Teacher Education at Calvin Colege, 1900-1930: And Gladly Teach**
19. Célestin Freinet, **Education Through Work: A Model for Child-Centered Learning**, John Sivell (trans.)
20. John Sivell (ed.), **Freinet Pedagogy: Theory and Practice**
21. John Klapper, **Foreign-Language Learning Through Immersion**
22. Maurice Whitehead, **The Academies of the Reverend Bartholomew Booth in Georgian England and Revolutionary America**

23. Margaret D. Tannenbaum, **Concepts and Issues in School Choice**
24. Rose M. Duhon-Sells and Emma T. Pitts, **An Interdisciplinary Approach to Multicultural Teaching and Learning**
25. Robert E. Ward, **An Encyclopedia of Irish Schools, 1500-1800**
26. David A. Brodie, **A Reference Manual for Human Performance Measurement in the Field of Physical Education and Sports Sciences**
27. Xiufeng Liu, **Mathematics and Science Curriculum Change in the People's Republic of China**
28. Judith Evans Longacre, **The History of Wilson College 1868 to 1970**
29. Thomas E. Jordan, **The First Decade of Life, Volume I: Birth to Age Five**
30. Thomas E. Jordan, **The First Decade of Life, Volume II: The Child From Five to Ten Years**
31. Mary I. Fuller and Anthony J. Rosie (eds.), **Teacher Education and School Partnerships**
32. James J. Van Patten (ed.), **Watersheds in Higher Education**
33. K. (Moti) Gokulsing and Cornel DaCosta (eds.), **Usable Knowledges as the Goal of University Education: Innovations in the Academic Enterprise Culture**
34. Georges Duquette (ed.), **Classroom Methods and Strategies for Teaching at the Secondary Level**
35. Linda A. Jackson and Michael Murray, **What Students Really Think of Professors: An Analysis of Classroom Evaluation Forms at an American University**
36. Donald H. Parkerson and Jo Ann Parkerson, **The Emergence of the Common School in the U.S. Countryside**
37. Neil R. Fenske, **A History of American Public High Schools, 1890-1990: Through the Eyes of Principals**
38. Gwendolyn M. Duhon Boudreaux (ed.), **An Interdisciplinary Approach to Issues and Practices in Teacher Education**
39. John Roach, **A Regional Study of Yorkshire Schools 1500-1820**
40. V.J. Thacker, **Using Co-operative Inquiry to Raise Awareness of the Leadership and Organizational Culture in an English Primary School**
41. Elizabeth Monk-Turner, **Community College Education and Its Impact on Socioeconomic Status Attainment**
42. George A. Churukian and Corey R. Lock (eds.), **International Narratives on Becoming a Teacher Educator: Pathways to a Profession**
43. Cecilia G. Manrique and Gabriel G. Manrique, **The Multicultural or Immigrant Faculty in American Society**
44. James J. Van Patten (ed.), **Challenges and Opportunities for Education in the 21st Century**
45. Barry W. Birnbaum, **Connecting Special Education and Technology for the 21st Century**
46. J. David Knottnerus and Frédérique Van de Poel-Knottnerus, **The Social Worlds of Male and Female Children in the Nineteenth Century French Educational System: Youth, Rituals, and Elites**

47. Sandra Frey Stegman, **Student Teaching in the Choral Classroom: An Investigation of Secondary Choral Music Student Teachers' Perceptions of Instructional Successes and Problems as They Reflect on Their Music Teaching**
48. Gwendolyn M. Duhon and Tony Manson (eds.), **Preparation, Collaboration, and Emphasis on the Family in School Counseling for the New Millennium**
49. Katherina Danko-McGhee, **The Aesthetic Preferences of Young Children**
50. Jane Davis-Seaver, **Critical Thinking in Young Children**
51. Gwendolyn M. Duhon and Tony J. Manson (eds.), **Implications for Teacher Education – Cross-Ethnic and Cross-Racial Dynamics of Instruction**
52. Samuel Mitchell, **Partnerships in Creative Activities Among Schools, Artists and Professional Organizations Promoting Arts Education**
53. Loretta Niebur, **Incorporating Assessment and the National Standards for Music Education into Everyday Teaching**
54. Tony Del Valle, **Written Literacy Features of Three Puerto Rican Family Networks in Chicago: An Ethnographic Study**
55. Christine J. Villani and Colin C. Ward, **Violence and Non-Violence in the Schools: A Manual for Administration**
56. Michael Dallaire, **Contemplation in Liberation – A Method for Spiritual Education in the Schools**
57. Gwendolyn M. Duhon, **Problems and Solutions in Urban Schools**
58. Paul Grosch, **Recognition of the Spirit and Its Development as Legitimate Concerns of Education**
59. D. Antonio Cantu, **An Investigation of the Relationship Between Social Studies Teachers' Beliefs and Practice**
60. Loretta Walton Jaggers, Nanthalia W. McJamerson and Gwendolyn M. Duhon (eds.), **Developing Literacy Skills Across the Curriculum: Practical, Approaches, Creative Models, Strategies, and Resources**
61. Haim Gordon and Rivca Gordon, **Sartre's Philosophy and the Challenge of Education**
62. Robert D. Buchanan and Ruth Ann Roberts, **Performance-Based Evaluation for Certificated and Non-Certificated School Personnel: Standards, Criteria, Indicators, Models**
63. C. David Warner III, **Opinions of Administrators, Faculty, and Students Regarding Academic Freedom and Student Artistic Expression**
64. Robert D. Heslep, **A Philosophical Guide for Decision Making by Educators: Developing a Set of Foundational Principles**
65. Noel P. Hurley, **How You Speak Determines How You Learn: Resource Allocation and Student Achievement**
66. Barry W. Birnbaum, **Foundations and Practices in the Use of Distance Education**
67. Franklin H. Silverman and Robert Moulton, **The Impact of a Unique Cooperative American University USAID Funded Speech-Language Pathologist, Audiologist, and Deaf Educator B.S. Degree Program in the Gaza Strip**
68. Tony J. Manson (ed.), **Teacher Education Preparation for Diversity**
69. Scott D. Robinson, **Autobiostories Promoting Emotional Insights into the Teaching and Learning of Secondary Science**

70. Francis Oakley, **The Leadership Challenge of a College Presidency: Meaning, Occasion, and Voice**
71. Melvin D. Williams, **The Ethnography of an Anthropology Department, 1959-1979: An Academic Village**
72. Kevin McGuinness, **The Concept of Academic Freedom**
73. Alastair Sharp, **Reading Comprehension and Text Organization**
74. Nicholas Beattie, **The Freinet Movements of France, Italy, and Germany, 1920-2000: Versions of Educational Progressivism**
75. Anne P. Chapman, **Language Practices in School Mathematics: A Social Semiotic Approach**
76. Wendy Robinson, **Pupil Teachers and Their Professional Training in Pupil-Teacher Centres in England and Wales, 1870-1914**
77. Barbara A. Sposet, **The Affective and Cognitive Development of Culture Learning During the Early and Middle Childhood Curriculum**
78. John P. Anchan and Shiva S. Halli, **Exploring the Role of the Internet in Global Education**
79. James J. Van Patten and Timothy J. Bergen, **A Case Study Approach to a Multi-Cultural Mosaic in Education**
80. Jeffrey L. Hoogeveen, **The Role of Students in the History of Composition**
81. Rose M. Duhon-Sells and Leslie Agard-Jones (eds.), **Educators Leading the Challenge to Alleviate School Violence**
82. Rose Marie Duhon-Sells, Halloway C. Sells, Alice Duhon-Ross, Gwendolyn Duhon, Glendolyn Duhon-JeanLouis (eds.) **International Perspectives on Methods of Improving Education Focusing on the Quality of Diversity**
83. Ruth Rees, **A New Era in Educational Leadership—One Principal, Two Schools: Twinning**
84. Daniel J. Mahoney, **An Organizational, Social-Psychological, and Ethical Analysis of School Administrators' Use of Deception**
85. Judith Longacre, **The Trial and Renewal of Wilson College**
86. Michael Delucchi, **Student Satisfaction with Higher Education During the 1970s—A Decade of Social Change**
87. Samuel Mitchell, **The Value of Educational Partnerships Worldwide with the Arts, Science, Business, and Community Organizations**
88. Susan Davis Lenski and Wendy L. Black (eds.), **Transforming Teacher Education Through Partnerships**
89. Ana Maria Klein, **Learning How Children Process Mathematical Problems**
90. Laura Shea Doolan, **The History of the International Learning Styles Network and Its Impact on Educational Innovation**
91. Gail Singleton Taylor (ed.), **The Impact of High-Stakes Testing on the Academic Futures of Non-Mainstream Students**
92. G.R. Evans, **Inside the University of Cambridge in the Modern World**
93. Agnes D. Walkinshaw, **Integrating Drama with Primary and Junior Education: The Ongoing Debate**
94. Joe Marshall Hardin and Ray Wallace (eds.), **Teaching, Research, and Service in the Twenty-First Century English Department: A Delicate Balance**

95. Samuel Mitchell, Patricia Klinck, and John Burger (eds.), **Worldwide Partnerships for Schools with Voluntary Organizations, Foundations, Universities, Companies, and Community Councils**
96. Emerson D. Case, **Making the Transition from an Intensive English Program to Mainstream University Courses–An Ethnographic Study**
97. Roberta A. McKay and Susan E. Gibson, **Social Studies for the 21st Century–A Review of Current Literature and Research**
98. Edith Sue Kohner Burford, **Investigating the Reasons University Students in the South Central United States Have to Retake First-Year English Composition**
99. Christina Isabelli-García, **A Case Study of the Factors in the Development of Spanish Linguistic Accuracy and Oral Communication Skills: Motivation and Extended Interaction in the Study Abroad Context**